ONE GREAT HOUR OF SHARING

Serve one another.

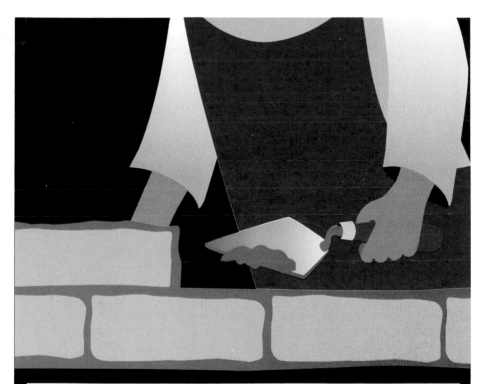

"Serve one another with whatever gift each of you has received."
—1 Peter 4:10b, NRSV

UNITED METHODIST
Your Gift Makes a World of Difference
SPECIAL SUNDAYS

D0000943

ONE GREAT HOUR OF SHARING

Serve one another.

Hands skillfully build; friends share a bowl of rice.
Some nurture; some plant.
Some sit at desks; some work outside; some travel worldwide.
Millions of people, each with a gift.

**"Serve one another with whatever gift
each of you has received."
—1 Peter 4:10b, NRSV**

Joining together to offer our gifts,
Joining together with those who struggle,
We build; we feed; we nurture.
We plant; we teach; we learn.

Together we recover—
from hatred unleashed worldwide
and the horror of nature's fury.
Together we offer sustenance—
to hungry people in Siberia
and uprooted masses in Afghanistan, Pakistan and Tajikistan.
Together, we offer hope—
to victims of economic crises in Nigeria
and displaced and refugee children everywhere.
Together we create a better life—
through mother and child health ministries in Europe,
agricultural programs in the Caribbean
and outreach to immigrants in the United States.

Together, through UMCOR and One Great Hour of Sharing,
We serve one another with God's abundant gifts.

People around the world depend on UMCOR,
and UMCOR depends on your One Great Hour of Sharing offering.
Please give generously. Your gift makes a world of difference!

**UNITED METHODIST COMMITTEE ON RELIEF
GENERAL BOARD OF GLOBAL MINISTRIES
THE UNITED METHODIST CHURCH**

**http://gbgm-umc.org/umcor
www.UMCGiving.org**

100141/2.6M/902

PRODUCED FOR THE CHURCH BY
UMCom
united methodist
communications

O Say Can You See?

JAMES W. MOORE

O Say Can You See?

Biblical Stories About Spiritual
Blindness

DIMENSIONS
FOR LIVING

NASHVILLE

O SAY CAN YOU SEE?
BIBLICAL STORIES ABOUT SPIRITUAL BLINDNESS

Copyright © 2000 by Dimensions for Living

This book is printed on acid-free paper.

Library of Congress Cataloging-in-Publication Data

Moore, James W. (James Wendell), 1938-
  O say can you see? : biblical stories about spiritual blindness / James W. Moore.
      p. cm.
  ISBN 0-687-09960-9 (alk. paper)
  1. Spiritual life—Biblical teaching. I. Title.

BS680.S7 .M66 2000
248.2—dc21

00-059619

02 03 04 05 06 07 08 09—10 9 8 7 6 5 4

MANUFACTURED IN THE UNITED STATES OF AMERICA

For June, Jodi and Danny,
Jeff and Claire, and
Sarah, Paul, and Dawson

And with appreciation to Cynthia Sarver,
Alta Mae Graves, and Joanne Mueller

Contents

Introduction

O Say Can You See?
Biblical Stories About
Spiritual Blindness

Recently, I asked a friend in the medical profession to give me a good definition of what a cataract is. The description of a cataract given to me by my friend was even better and more help ful than I had expected it to be. Here's the definition: (As you read it, think about what might be "spiritual cataracts" for us.)

"In medical terms, a cataract is a clouding over of the lens of the eye. This 'filminess' causes a loss of transparency causing 'distorted vision.' There is no pain; the loss of vision is gradual: it slips up on you. The cataract abnormality may occur in younger people as a result of some trauma, but most commonly occurs in adults. If left unattended, the cloudiness may become so heavy that no light can get through at all and vision is lost altogether. Cataracts can be removed by surgery."

There's a lesson in this somewhere, isn't there?

This medical description brings to mind the words of Jesus in Matthew 6:22-23*a* (RSV) as he says: "The eye is the lamp of the body. So, if your eye is sound, your whole body will be full of light; but if your eye is not sound, your whole body will be full of darkness."

It is interesting to note here that in the Greek language (which was the original language of the New Testament) the word *body* meant more than the physical anatomy. Rather, it meant what we today would call the total personality.

With that in mind, let me paraphrase Jesus: The eye is the lamp of the total personality; or in other words, the way we see things, the way we look at things, the way we view things, the perspective we bring to things says a lot about us and our spiritual lives. The way we view our job, material things, the world, life says a lot about our spiritual health.

Remember that episode in the old *Andy Griffith Show* when Barney Fife, the nervous deputy of Mayberry, decides to become an amateur psychiatrist. He sends off for an amateur psychiatric kit. When it arrives, he tries it out on Otis, the town character. Using the classic "inkblot test," Barney shows Otis one of the "ink blots" and says, "Look at this, Otis, and tell me what you see!" Otis answers, "I see a bat!" Barney gets upset and says, "That's the difference between you and me, Otis! You see a bat and I see a butterfly!"

Well, for once in his life, Barney was precisely on target: The difference between people is indeed often most clearly demonstrated by the way we see things. The poet put it like this: "Two men looked out prison bars, one saw mud; the other saw stars."

When Jesus implies that we should "beware of spiritual cataracts," he is reminding us that there are certain obvious things that can blind our eyes—or cloud and distort our vision. The point is clear: Every now and then we need to have our eyes checked. How is our spiritual vision? How are we seeing things? Are we seeing clearly? Or do we have "spiritual cataracts," which are distorting our vision? Do we need a "second touch" from the Great Physician to heal us from our fuzzy vision.

America's national anthem begins with the simple question, "O Say Can You See?" Interestingly there is a remarkable section of scripture in the Gospel of Mark that raises this same question, "O Say Can You See?" It begins in the middle of the eighth chapter of Mark (verse 32) and continues all the way through chapter 10.

It's about spiritual blindness. If you turn in your Bible to Mark 8:22, you will discover that this fascinating section of scripture begins with the healing of a man who is blind, who sees at first, but not clearly. He says: "I can see people, but they look like trees, walking." Jesus has to touch him again before he can see clearly. That's how this amazing section of scripture begins, and then it ends in chapter 10:46-52 with the healing of Bartimaeus, who was also blind.

All the material in between has to do with different kinds of spiritual blindness. We see here the blindness of prejudice, narrowness, arrogance, jealousy, self-importance, mixed-up priorities, selfish ambition, and exclusiveness.

Now, look with me at this powerful section of scripture. First, you will notice that there is the prelude in Mark 8:22-26, and be sure to notice the uniqueness of this opening miracle. It happens gradually! It's the only miracle of Jesus that happens gradually. At Bethsaida, Jesus touches the man who is blind and at first his vision is not clear. It is better, it is improved; but still his vision is fuzzy. Jesus touches him again and now he can see everything clearly.

Now, this "fuzzy vision" is symbolic of what is to follow. As this material in Mark's Gospel unfolds, we see a lot of fuzzy vision—people trying to see clearly, but they have blind spots. Their vision is muddled, confused, unclear. They desperately need a second touch from the Master to clear up the blind spots, to sharpen the focus, to wipe away the blurred images.

Here is a brief overview of what is before us:

- *In Mark 8:27-33* we discover Simon Peter seeing the truth at Caesarea Philippi and yet not quite. He is so near but yet so far. He is tripped up and blinded by his own prejudice.
- *In Mark 9:2-8* we find the powerful and awesome Transfiguration experience, and here again Simon Peter sees the truth and yet still he has fuzzy vision. He doesn't quite get it. This time he is blinded by his own narrowness.
- *In Mark 9:33 and 34* we find the disciples walking down the road behind Jesus. He is heading steadfastly toward the cross, thinking deep thoughts about what awaits him in Jerusalem and all the while the disciples are strolling along behind him squabbling and arguing and backbiting. And—are you ready for this? They are fussing about which one of them is the greatest—a not-so-pretty picture of the blindness of arrogance.
- *In Mark 9:38-41* John (of all people) displays the blindness of jealousy, as he wants to stop a man from preaching because the man is not in their group.

- *In Mark 10:13-16* we see the fuzzy vision of the disciples as they try to hold the little children back and keep them away from Jesus. And, of course, you remember how Jesus said: "No, no, no. Don't do that. Let the children come. Bring them here to me." This story shows how the disciples were blinded by their own self-importance.
- *In Mark 10:17-22* you will recognize immediately that this is the famous story of the rich young ruler who turned away sadly from the Master's call, blinded by his mixed-up priorities.
- *In Mark 10:35-40* we find James and John in their blind ambition trying to get ahead of the other disciples (especially Simon Peter) as they ask for the top two spots in the new Kingdom.
- Then this fascinating section of scripture ends *in Mark 10:46-52* with the story of Bartimaeus who is healed by Jesus and (who in contrast to the rich young ruler) drops everything and immediately follows Jesus on the way.

In this book, we will take a look at these eight great stories from Mark's Gospel and then examine how the good news of the Christian faith "opens our eyes" to see more clearly the abundant life God gives us through Christ. In addition, there are epilogues, titled "O Say Can America See?" that raise two crucial and timely topics: "The Demoralizing of America" and "The Answer for America."

It is my hope and prayer that as we examine these powerful sections of scripture, God will touch our eyes afresh, clear away the blind spots, take away the spiritual cataracts, and sharpen our focus so that we may see life with the eyes of faith and, indeed, with the eyes of Christ.

1

The Blindness of Prejudice

Jesus went on with his disciples to the villages of
Caesarea Philippi; and on the way he asked his disciples, "Who do people say that I am?" And they
answered him, "John the Baptist; and others, Elijah;
and still others, one of the prophets." He asked them,
"But who do you say that I am?" Peter answered him,
"You are the Messiah." And he sternly ordered them
not to tell anyone about him. Then he began to teach
them that the Son of Man must undergo great suffering, and be rejected by the elders, the chief priests, and
the scribes, and be killed, and after three days rise
again. He said all this quite openly. And Peter took
him aside and began to rebuke him. But turning and
looking at his disciples, he rebuked Peter and said,
"Get behind me, Satan! For you are setting your mind
not on divine things but on human things."
—Mark 8:27-33

Alfred Henry Lewis once told a colorful cowboy story that
demonstrates dramatically that it is risky and wrong to judge a person who's acting in a strange or unusual way, if you don't know
the reason for the person's behavior.

Back in the late part of the nineteenth century and the early part
of the twentieth century, Alfred Henry Lewis wrote several books
about the exploits and experiences of some of the early

cowboys in the Wild West. Most of the fictitious stories were told in the voice of the Old Cattleman (O.C. for short) who lived through some rawhide times in the frontier town of Wolfville, Arizona.

The Wolfville books are fascinating in their own right, but on top of that some of them were illustrated by a pretty fair cowboy artist named Frederic Remington. The story about blindly judging the actions of others is in the book, *Faro Nell and Her Friends,* published in 1913 by G. W. Dillingham in New York. Here's the story.

O.C. and his friend, Steve, were camped out in the western hills when they were suddenly confronted by an angry buffalo. The buffalo obviously meant to do them harm. To escape the buffalo, O.C. climbed what he described as a measly pinion tree, but Steve—with no other choice— dived into a cave with the buffalo's horns within inches of his backside.

Now, here's the strange part: A few seconds after Steve had dived to safety in the cave, he suddenly popped back out of the cave to face the buffalo again. This made the buffalo even angrier, and he charged again; and once again Steve dived back into the cave. Soon as the buffalo would turn his back to leave, here would come Steve again running back out of the cave.

The buffalo would turn and charge, and Steve would again dive back into the cave. This went on several times. The buffalo bull would charge; Steve would dive into the cave. The buffalo would turn away, and Steve would pop back out of the cave; the buffalo would charge once more, and Steve would dive back into the cave.

Now, O.C. was up in his tree watching all of this and at last he yelled down to Steve, "Steve, have you lost your mind? Why don't you just stay in the cave until the buffalo gives up and goes away?"

Steve yelled back, "It's well and good for you to ask that question sitting all safe up there in your tree. But what you don't know about this cave is there's a bear in it!"

Now, the point of that story is clear. When we see a person behaving in a way that we think is strange, before we jump to our own conclusions and we judge that person harshly, we ought to be aware that that person might be in a hole and there might be a bear in there with him. (Thanks to Leon Hale for reminding me of this famous old story in his *Houston Chronicle* column 10-9-97.)

There are lots of people who have "bears in their caves," bears that we can't see; and to judge people without the whole truth is wrong. It is also the perfect setup for misjudging people, events, and situations. Something like this happened to Simon Peter at Caesarea Philippi.

Remember the story in Mark 8. Jesus asked his disciples, "Who do the people say that I am? What's the talk out in the fields and in the streets and in the marketplace?"

And they told him, "Some say you are John the Baptist and others say Elijah and others say one of the prophets."

Then Jesus asked that question that has resounded across the ages: "But who do you say that I am?" And Simon Peter answered, "You are the Christ!"

"Good answer, Simon Peter," we say to ourselves; and we feel that Peter sees it—but look what happened next.

Jesus went on to tell how he must suffer and be rejected and crucified and resurrected. Simon Peter rebukes him. Perhaps feeling a bit cocky from his earlier good answer, now Peter takes it upon himself to straighten Jesus out.

"No! Master! You can't do it that way. You've got it all mixed up. That's not the way for a Messiah to act. Messiahs don't suffer. They conquer! Messiahs are powerful and violent and nationalistic and destructive and vengeful. Look, Lord, I know you mean well, but surely you are not serious about this suffering business. That's simply no way for a Messiah to act. You're probably just tired. I can't let you go through with this! I won't let you go through with this. People will think you have lost your mind!"

Then Jesus turns and says to Simon Peter, "Get thee behind me, Satan! When you talk like that you are not on the side of God!"

Tough words, hard words—what are we to make of this? Well, you see, the problem here is that Simon Peter is blinded by his prejudice. He doesn't know the whole story. He doesn't see the complete picture. He doesn't have all the facts. He had prejudged how the Savior should act, and he doesn't want Jesus to break out of that box. He had prejudged what the Savior should do; and he was blind to any new idea, blind to any other way.

That's how prejudice affects us, isn't it? It blinds us. It narrows our sight. It distorts and blurs our vision. It stifles our perceptions. It fuzzies up our seeing.

When Jesus connected messiahship with suffering and death, it blew Simon Peter's mind. That's why Peter protested so violently. He was locked up, bound, and blinded by his own prejudice. In effect, he was crying out those famous words, "Wait a minute, Lord, we never did it that way before."

So, here at Caesarea Philippi we see it: the blindness of prejudice. Here we see dramatically the distorted vision that inevitably comes whenever we try to judge people or critique someone's actions:

- when we don't know the whole truth,
- when we don't have access to all the information,
- when we can't see the complete picture,
- when we can't see the bears in their caves.

In this powerful Caesarea Philippi story in Mark 8, we see clearly outlined for us the problem with prejudice. Now, of course, sadly we all have seen the horrendous ugliness of prejudice in news stories, in the papers and on television, about radical hate groups and vicious hate crimes that are so cruel and so sick that they turn our stomachs and break our hearts. But, here in this story we see another scary side of prejudice, namely that it can slip up on the best of people and blind us in at least three ways:

- it can cause us to be lazy and harsh;
- it can cause us to misjudge people and events;
- and, it can cause us to be closed-minded.

First, Prejudice Can Slip Up on the Best of People and Can Cause Us to Be Lazy and Harsh

What is the message in this story for you and me? What is the take-home value? What does this all mean for you and me right here and right now?

Well, we learn here that the blindness of prejudice can take root in good people. Simon Peter was one of the best. He was the obvious leader of the disciple group, highly regarded by Jesus, looked up to by the others; and yet, prejudice caused this good man to have blind spots!

There's a message there somewhere, and the message is this: It can happen to you and me! Prejudice can slip in and give us fuzzy vision. It can blind us.

One of my professors put it bluntly. He said, "Prejudice is the sin of ignorance born of laziness." It is being unwilling to take the time and give the effort to seek and find the truth.

Abraham Maslow said the same thing like this, "If the only tool you have is a hammer . . . you tend to treat everything as if it were a nail."

But really, prejudice is just what the word says. It is the sin of prejudging! It's judging someone:

- without really knowing them,
- without really knowing the facts,
- without knowing the complete story,
- without knowing the person as a person.

Some years ago when I left Tennessee to go to seminary in Ohio, I was a little nervous about going "up north" for the first time. My first day on campus I met a student from Michigan. When he heard that I was a "Southerner from Tennessee," he immediately became very hostile.

"A Southerner, huh!" he said with anger. "I know about you people! You should be ashamed of yourself! I know how you treat minority groups! I know about your prejudice!"

Well, that hurt to be verbally attacked like that, and it made me mad too. But, somehow I was able to maintain my composure; and I said quietly, "Do you know what the word *prejudice* means?" "Of course I do," he retorted. "It means to prejudge, to label people, to write them off, to judge them negatively without really knowing them."

"That's right," I answered, "and I think that's what you just did to me."

There was a moment of silence. He looked at me fiercely, and I thought for an instant that maybe I had gone too far. But then his face softened and he replied, "I believe you are right, and I think I owe you an apology. I'm sorry." He put out his hand, and I shook it. From that moment, we became close friends and still are.

Prejudice is a terrible thing. To lump people into groups is blind and unfair and often vicious. To think all musicians are alike, to think all women are alike, to think all Southerners or Northerners are alike is wrong! To lump all artists or all young people or all people over thirty into a group is unfair. To imagine that all teachers, or all psychiatrists, or all African Americans, or all Latinos, or all Asians, or all redheaded people are the same is blind and wrong. At best, it is narrow stereotyping. At worst, it is heartbreaking cruelty.

Prejudice distorts our vision because it will not look at new ways or new facts or new possibilities. It is lazy, it is sinful, it's harsh, and it is unchristian. It blinds us to the uniqueness and individuality of each of God's children. Prejudice is a spiritual cataract. To prejudge other people is cruel. To prejudge God is profane.

So, here at Caesarea Philippi we see it. The blindness of prejudice, how it can make us lazy and harsh; and we hear strongly from the lips of Jesus the warning that when we are prejudiced we are not on the side of God!

Second, the Blindness of Prejudice Can Slip Up on the Best of People and Can Cause Us to Misjudge People and Events

In his autobiography, Mahatma Gandhi wrote that during his student days even though he was a Hindu, he was fascinated with Christianity. He read the Gospels seriously. He was so impressed with the life and teachings of Jesus that he considered converting to Christianity. He believed that in the teachings of Jesus he could find the solution to the caste system that was dividing, separating, and hurting the people of India.

So one Sunday he decided to attend services at a nearby

Christian church. He planned to participate in the worship service and then after church talk to the minister about becoming a Christian. However, one member of the church saw him coming, thought he looked suspicious, decided that he was a troublemaker, and stopped him as he entered the sanctuary.

The man blocked his way at the door. The man told Gandhi that he should go worship with his own people, that he would be much more comfortable with his own kind. Mahatma Gandhi (because of the prejudice of that one man) left the church and never returned. "If Christians have caste differences also," he said, "I might as well remain a Hindu."

That man who turned Gandhi away had been blinded by prejudice. His prejudice caused him to completely misjudge the man and his motives. His prejudice caused him to betray a sincere seeker, to betray the church, to betray our faith, and to betray our Christ. You know as well as I do that Christ would have welcomed him with open arms.

Put that over against this. A short time after the War Between the States, a church in Washington, D.C. was celebrating Holy Communion. As the minister called the people to come to the altar to receive the sacrament, suddenly the backdoor of the church opened and an African American man who was a former slave walked in, came down the center aisle, and knelt at the altar.

This had never happened before. African Americans and slaves had come to the church, had even been members; but they always stayed up in the balcony. The congregation sat there stunned. Tensions were still high. No one seemed to know what to do. Then one white man stood up, walked to the altar, and knelt right beside the former slave. The minister served them Communion, others came, and the service went on. After the service the white man was questioned about his actions. "How could you do that?" one outraged man asked. He answered, "My friend, all ground is level beneath the cross." Oh, by the way, the white man's name you might recognize; he was a devout Christian whose name was General Robert E. Lee! Prejudice is so dangerous because it can cause us to be lazy and harsh, and it can cause us to misjudge people and events.

Third, Prejudice Can Slip Up on the Best of People and Can Cause Us to Be Closed-Minded

On February 12, 2000, I was having lunch with some friends. Someone came to the table and said, "Have you heard the news? Charles Schulz died last night." The gasps around the table would not have been more audible if it were a neighbor or a friend. That's what Charles Schulz was to all of us, a friend and neighbor:

someone to depend on in the morning paper,
someone to chuckle with over some weakness or foible we have all experienced,
someone who could draw our picture with the attendant insecurities through his lovable "Peanuts" characters,
someone who could expose our sins in a way that made us want to be better.

Charles Schulz knew about the sin of the closed mind. One Sunday he depicted it like this,

Lucy was chasing Charlie Brown, shouting, "I'll get you Charlie Brown. I'll catch you; and when I do, I'm going to knock your block off!"

Suddenly, Charlie Brown screeched to a halt. He turned around and said, "Wait a minute, Lucy. If you and I as relatively small children with relatively small problems can't sit down and talk through our problems in a mature way, how can we expect the nations of the world to?" Then POW! Lucy slugged him and said, "I had to hit him quick, he was beginning to make sense."

That is exactly what they did to Jesus! They hit him quick with a cross because he was beginning to make sense. In my opinion, nothing was more responsible for nailing Jesus to a cross than the sin of the closed mind, and that's why Jesus responded so strongly to Simon Peter when he saw the sin of the closed mind slipping up on him.

Now, the good news here is this: Simon Peter (like the blind man at Bethsaida) received a second touch. He got redeemed! He got healed! Later, as Jesus touched him again, he saw clearly; and he became one of the great visionary leaders of the early church, indeed, one of the great visionary leaders of all time!

Let me ask you something. Can you see clearly right now? Do you need a second touch? If so, the doctor is in the house! The Great Physician is here, nearer than breathing, closer than hands and feet, and he can make you whole. He can open your eyes and make you see.

2

The Blindness of Narrowness

Six days later, James took with him Peter and James and John, and led them up a high mountain apart, by themselves. And he was transfigured before them, and his clothes became dazzling white, such as no one on earth could bleach them. And there appeared to them Elijah with Moses, who were talking with Jesus. Then Peter said to Jesus, "Rabbi, it is good for us to be here; let us make three dwellings, one for you, one for Moses, and one for Elijah." He did not know what to say, for they were terrified. Then a cloud overshadowed them, and from the cloud there came a voice, "This is my Son, the Beloved; listen to him!" Suddenly when they looked around, they saw no one with them any more, but only Jesus.

—Mark 9:2-8

One of the greatest things that can be said about our Christian faith is that it combines devotional life with social action. Through worship and service, on the mountain and in the valley, we reach up to God and out to others. We see this dramatically in the scripture for this chapter because in the Transfiguration story, we see beautifully outlined three different approaches to religion.

First, there are the Pietists, symbolized here by Simon Peter. They say, "Let's just stay up here on this mountaintop. Let's just stay here and worship and not get smudged by the problems of the world."

Second, there are the social activists, symbolized here by the other disciples. They are down in the valley trying to heal, but they can't do it because they have no power; they have no power because they haven't been up on the mountain.

Third, there is the approach of Jesus. He combines the first two. He puts worship and service together. He puts devotion and social action together. He goes up on the mountain to worship and then comes down into the valley to heal.

The message is clear: Don't be blinded by narrowness. Don't try to separate the devotional life from social action. They go together. That's what this great passage Mark 9:2-8 teaches us. It also reminds us of the great safety rules for the soul. Let me show you what I mean.

Early on in life we are all taught important safety rules. At home, in church, and in school, we learn these valuable safety rules that serve us well, protect us, and hopefully stay with us for a lifetime. "Don't hit!" "Don't push!" "Don't throw things!" "Don't jaywalk!" "Don't ever take medicine without first reading the label!" "Don't run with a pointed object in your hand!"

My dad, who liked to tease, used to say to us children, "Don't ever put anything in your ear, but your elbow!" (And we would try that.) And then there is that significant guideline from The Muppets' Miss Piggy, who says, "Don't ever eat anything that's bigger than you!"

Of course, the most widely known safety rule is "*Stop, Look, and Listen* before you cross the street." That's good advice when you come to a busy intersection. It is also a profound guideline for spiritual living. It's a good, helpful "safety rule for the soul."

That is precisely what Jesus is doing here in Mark 9 as he goes up on the Mount of Transfiguration. Jesus has come to a crucial intersection in his life. He is ready to "set his face toward Jerusalem" (compare Luke 9:53), to head toward that showdown in the Holy City. He goes up on the mountain to stop, look, and listen before he heads to the cross.

Remember the story with me.

Jesus has had a very popular and successful ministry in Galilee. He has been healing people, helping people, inspiring people, and comforting people, and great crowds are coming out to see him, hear him, and touch him. Everything's going great in Galilee, but not so in Jerusalem. Jesus knows how people are being abused, mistreated, and exploited by the Temple authorities down in Jerusalem. The authorities are getting rich at the expense of the common folk. Jesus sees how wrong this is. His heart goes out to the people as he sees how they are being tricked and cheated in the name of religion. The Temple of God has become a den of robbers. Instead of praying to God, the authorities are now *prey*ing on the people.

Jesus can't stand this, and he is determined to go down there and "strike a blow for justice." He is determined to go to Jerusalem and "lay his life on the line" for the people. But before he does that, before he makes that journey, before he steps out into that busy street, before he crosses that crucial intersection, he goes up on the mountain to stop, look, and listen!

Jesus takes Peter, James, and John along with him, and they have an incredible "mountaintop experience." This may well be where that phrase "mountaintop experience" comes from. Something quite wonderful, mysterious, and miraculous happened there, something too big for words. We can only bow in reverence as we try to understand it.

Peter, James, and John were touched, inspired, and visibly shaken by what they saw: Moses and Elijah were there with Jesus on the mountaintop! What on earth could this mean? So many things. This story is packed full of powerful symbols.

In the Scriptures, the mountain represents Nearness to God. The cloud represents the Presence of God. The light represents the Truth of God. Moses represents the Law; he was the supreme lawgiver. Elijah represents the Prophets; he was the first and greatest of the prophets.

So what the Transfiguration experience says to us is this: All the biblical faith that has gone before is now summed up in Jesus and his message of love. It has all come to fruition in him. The law and the prophets come together in Jesus. The law and the prophets are fulfilled in Jesus. Jesus goes up on the mountain to think through his trip to Jerusalem, to think through his journey to the cross, and there in the presence of God the Father, Moses, the lawgiver, and Elijah the prophet, the message resounds across that mountaintop: "Go for it!" "Go on!" "Do it!" "Go to Jerusalem and stand tall for what is right!" "Go to the Holy City and lay your life on the line for the people!"

Jesus had already made the decision to go, but there on the Mount of Transfiguration, his decision was confirmed dramatically. He went up on the mountain to stop, look, and listen—and then he came down and "set his face toward Jerusalem!" That's what a spiritual experience does for us. We go up to the mountaintop; we stop, we look, we listen; we experience the presence of God and the witness of those who have gone before us—and empowered by that, we go down into the valley to serve.

Do you know what Jesus does when he comes down from the mountain? The first thing he does is heal a little boy who has epilepsy (see Mark 9:14-29). This magnificent story has within it some great safety rules for the soul that we would do well to observe constantly. They are so simple, but oh so profound—the importance of taking the time to stop, look, and listen before we go. Let's take a look at these one at a time.

First, We Stop

It is so important to stop every now and then—to slow up, center down, and focus in. Have you ever noticed in a football game—as active and as hectic as that is—even in a football game, they stop after every play! They huddle, they rest, they refresh. They think about where they are, where they want to go, what they need to do, and what play they need to call before going back to the line of scrimmage. Now, for the football purists, let me hurry to say that I know about the hurry-up offense and the no-huddle offense. But, even when they don't huddle, still—even then—they stop, and the quarterback gives the offense instructions as they wait and catch their breath and get ready to run the next play.

The point is clear: Every now and then in the game of life we need to stop and refocus; we need to stop and smell the roses; we need to stop and celebrate the presence of God. The Bible makes it clear that there is a rhythm to life—a rhythm of work and worship, labor and rest. An old Greek proverb puts it like this: "The bow that is always bent will finally cease to shoot at all."

In Thornton Wilder's great play *Our Town,* Emily, the young woman who has died, is permitted to return to her home in Grover's Corners to relive one day with her family. She chooses the day of her twelfth birthday, but she is very disappointed by the whole experience. Everyone is just too busy. Everyone is too preoccupied. She pleads with her brothers and sisters and her father and mother to stop, to stop and touch one another, to stop and experience one another, to stop and celebrate one another and hug one another—but nobody stops. They are too caught up in the busyness of life. Emily realizes how harried, how harassed, how anxious, and how empty they all are. And finally, Emily cries out in despair: "Take me away! Take me away!" And as the Stage Manager leads her back toward heaven, Emily says this, "Do any human beings ever realize life while they live it?"

You know what Emily was saying? She was saying, Why don't people stop anymore? Why don't people stop and celebrate life and experience one another? Why don't people stop and feel the warm presence of God? Let me ask you something: How are *you* doing with this? Are you stopping every now and then to let your soul catch up with your body? This is the first safety rule for the soul. Every now and then, we need to stop and spend some quiet time with God. First we stop.

Second, We Look

Safety rule number two: We look. We open our eyes and really see what's happening around us. Peter, James, and John opened their eyes on the Mount of Transfiguration, and they saw incredible things all about them; they saw the miracles of God.

One morning, some years ago, an artist was walking along a beautiful seashore with a group of friends. The artist was pointing out to the group the different things she was seeing—on the horizon, in the breaking of the waves on the shoreline, in the cloud formations in the sky—things she was seeing in the water and on the sand and in the textures and shadings of light.

A little girl playing in the sand nearby heard the artist's fascinating descriptions of what she was seeing; and the little girl stopped what she was doing, ran over to the artist, and said, "Wait a minute! Please wait. Don't say another word. Let me go and get my mother so she can see this too. I won't be long, we just live right there."

The artist said, "Oh, I'm sure your mother has seen all of this many, many times before."

"But she's never seen it like this," said the little girl. "I want her to see it all through your eyes."

Wouldn't it be something if you and I could learn how to see life through the eyes of Christ. How perceptive he was! He could walk through a field and see wheat and flowers, seeds and sunsets, birds and lambs and children, and all of them would speak to him of God. Or he would walk into the crowded streets of Jericho and see Zacchaeus up in that sycamore tree, or see an outcast who no one else seemed to notice. When we see things through the eyes of Jesus Christ, we can see people to help, problems to solve, blessings to count. It's a valuable safety rule for our souls. First, we stop. Second, we look.

Third, We Listen

A mother and her small daughter were looking at dolls in a department store one day. "What does it do?" the child would ask about each doll.

The mother would answer, "It walks" or "it talks" or "it sleeps" or "this one sings" and "this one cries."

The dolls were rather expensive, so the mother tried to direct her little girl's interest toward an ordinary doll that was more reasonably priced.

"But does it *do* anything?" the child asked.

"Oh, yes," the mother replied, "it does one of the best

things of all—it listens!" The little girl eagerly reached for that doll.

We like someone who listens. And so does God! Why is that so hard? Why is it so difficult for us to settle down, to tune in, and to listen?

Just a few weeks after the McCaughey septuplets were born, I heard a fascinating interview. A local radio station was interviewing the grandmother of the septuplets. The grandmother was asked if she could recognize all seven of the babies and recall which name went with which. "Oh, yes," she said, "they already have their own little personalities." And then she said something amazing. She said, "The mother of the septuplets can be in another room and hear the babies crying and can tell you which one or which two or which three are crying. She is so tuned in that she can recognize the cries and coos of each individual baby."

Now, think of that. Wouldn't it be something if we could tune in to listen and to hear the voice of God with the same intensity and sensitivity that a good mother has for hearing her baby? These are essential safety rules for the soul—to stop, to look, and to listen.

Now, I had planned to have three points in this chapter—Stop, Look, and Listen—but then I realized I couldn't end here, because there is another part of this. When you come to an intersection, you stop, you look, you listen, and when you've done *these* three things, *then* what do you do?

You Go!

You step out into the streets of life. You go into the world to serve and help and heal. That is precisely what Jesus did in Mark 9:2-8, 14-29. He went up on the mountain, and then, empowered by that spiritual experience, he immediately went down into the valley and healed a little boy who was very sick.

You remember the old story of the man who comes to church late one Sunday morning? He rushes into the outer foyer, and he sees the head usher there, and he says to him, "Is the service over?" And the usher answers wisely, "Well, the *worship* is over, but the *service* has just begun!"

Precisely so! We stop, we look, we listen—and then, empowered by that mountaintop experience, we go down into the valley to be God's servants, to be the instruments of God's healing power.

3

The Blindness of Arrogance

> They went on from there and passed through
> Galilee. He did not want anyone to know it; for he was
> teaching his disciples, saying to them, "The Son of
> Man is to be betrayed into human hands, and they will
> kill him, and three days after being killed, he will rise
> again." But they did not understand what he was say-
> ing and were afraid to ask him.
>   Then they came to Capernaum; and when he was in
> the house he asked them, "What were you arguing
> about on the way?" But they were silent, for on the
> way they had argued with one another who was the
> greatest. He sat down, called the twelve, and said to
> them, "Whoever wants to be first must be last of all
> and servant of all." Then he took a little child and put
> it among them; and taking it in his arms, he said to
> them, "Whoever welcomes one such child in my name
> welcomes me, and whoever welcomes me welcomes not
> me but the one who sent me."
>
> —*Mark 9:30-37*

Let me begin with a question. Be honest now.

Have you ever been reduced to an embarrassed silence—the
kind of silence that comes from a sense of shame, that comes from
doing wrong and being found out, that comes from suddenly

realizing that you have "shortcut" your best self? There is a haunting example of this kind of embarrassed silence in Mark's Gospel. Remember it?

Jesus is heading toward Jerusalem. He is heading toward the cross when his disciples begin to bicker and quarrel. They are arguing about which of them should be greatest in the Kingdom. Can you get the picture of this in your mind? There is something painfully heartbreaking to me in this scene. On the one hand, here is Jesus—moving steadfastly toward the cross; his face set toward Jerusalem; resolved, committed, surely thinking deep thoughts about the hard confrontation that was certain to come in the Holy City; determined to stand tall and firm and strong and do the Father's will, to strike a blow for justice, to face it all head-on, come what may.

Then on the other hand, here are the disciples walking along behind him—completely misunderstanding the Kingdom, thinking of it in simplistic, selfish, materialistic terms, and of themselves as the high-ranking, prestigious chiefs of state; bickering and fussing and quarreling over who should get the top spots, the most important positions. They are not aware that Jesus hears them, but he does! Then he stops. He turns and asks them, "By the way, what were you discussing along the road?" He knows, you see, and now with the question they know that he knows —and "they were silent!" Think about that heavy phrase "they were silent." They are reduced to the silence of shame, an embarrassed silence, so ashamed of their pettiness that they are speechless!

Isn't it fascinating how things take their proper place and acquire their true character when they are set before the eyes of Christ, when they are "played back" in the presence of Christ? So long as they thought Jesus was not hearing them, the argument about who should be greatest seemed fair enough; but when that argument had to be stated in Jesus' presence, it was exposed in all its unworthiness!

This raises some penetrating questions, doesn't it? If Christ knew what we were doing, would we be embarrassed? If Christ heard what we were saying, would we be ashamed? If Christ knew what we were thinking and feeling, would we be red-faced and speechless? Be candid with yourself for just a moment. Have you ever been reduced to an embarrassed, shameful silence? I guess if the truth were known, we all have.

I'm thinking of a group of people engaged in a rather cruel gossip session, talking harshly and critically about another person, when suddenly that person walks unannounced into the room—and there is an awkward, embarrassed silence. I'm thinking of some teenagers thumbing through some questionable literature, when suddenly Mother appears at the door—and there is an awkward, embarrassed silence. I'm thinking of a group of men exchanging shady stories, when suddenly right in the middle of one of the stories—perhaps at the most profane moment—someone they respect and admire greatly walks up unexpectedly—again, an awkward, shameful silence. I'm thinking of some office workers who are really loafing on the job, wasting valuable time, when suddenly the boss walks in and quietly, quickly, abashedly—they slip back into their workplaces.

Do any of these sound at all familiar? Being caught like this can be a very agonizing experience. How well we know that! When I was in the fourth grade at Hollywood Elementary School in Memphis, I had a "red-faced" moment like that which is still vivid and crystal clear in my memory. It happened in the school library. As fourth graders, we were being allowed more freedom in the library, and on this particular day as I was browsing around, my eyes fell on a strange book title. I couldn't believe it—a book in the Hollywood School library with the unmentionable "four-letter word" in its title. Remember now that this was in the late 1940s, and to see a four-letter word in print back then was shocking indeed!

As I pulled the book off the shelf and examined it, I understood what had happened. The real title of the book was *Hello, the Boat,* but somehow over the years the last letter in the word *Hello* (the *o*) had been rubbed out; and as a nine-year-old in the fourth grade, I thought it was hilarious—a four-letter word in the school library. Snickering, I began to motion for my friends and classmates to come over and share in this terrific scoop of mine. One-by-one they came and proudly I pointed out my discovery. We were giggling and snickering, when suddenly I felt a hand on my shoulder and heard a question, "What have you boys found over here that is so interesting?"

We turned and looked up into the face of Mrs. Smart, the librarian, and we were reduced to an embarrassed silence—especially me, because I had started it, because I was holding the book, and because not only was Mrs. Smart the librarian at school she was also my Sunday school teacher at church! I can remember the agony of that moment as if it were yesterday—my flushed face, my emotional pain, my embarrassment, and the feeling that Mrs. Smart was disappointed in me. I was totally speechless. I had no defense, no excuse, no explanation. I had been found out—and I was feeling the agony of being reduced to silence, the silence of shame.

Blow that up a bit, take it to a deeper level and you have something like what happened to the disciples in Capernaum that day as they traveled with Jesus on the road to Jerusalem. Let's examine this more closely by asking, What were the disciples doing, saying, feeling that later came back to haunt them? What attitudes were they expressing that later in the presence of Christ seemed so petty and so unworthy? What was it that reduced them to a shameful silence? Three things:

- ruthless pride,
- bitter self-centeredness, and
- bickering hostility.

Three things. Let's take a look at these. We may find ourselves somewhere between the lines.

First, They Were Reduced to Silence by Their Ruthless Pride

Now, of course, we know that there is a good kind of pride, a healthy pride. It's great to be proud of our children and our church and our heritage. It's good to be proud of our school and our city and our nation. It's obvious that pride can be a good quality in our lives. It only becomes bad when distorted or misused. When it becomes selfish and ruthless, then it becomes a spiritual poison. That's what was brewing in the disciple group that day. Each disciple was saying in his own prideful way: "I'm going to get ahead, come what may. If I have to elbow other people out of the way, then so be it!" Here it is, the picture of selfish, ruthless pride; and it is not a very pretty picture, is it?

In another place in Mark's Gospel, James and John have the audacity to ask Jesus for the top two places, the two best positions in his kingdom. We will develop this more specifically in chapter 7; but for now, just notice how James and John in a prideful way were trying to slip in ahead of the others, especially Simon Peter. They wanted to push in ahead of him. It's interesting to note that when Matthew told the same story later, he changed it a bit. He tried to soften it. He tried to clean up the act a bit, to cover for James and John and their ruthless pride.

But you can't really soften it. In the economy of God, the truth will come out and ruthless pride when it is uncovered and exposed will reduce you to a shameful silence. "Ruthless pride": I had a fascinating thought recently about that word *ruthless*. *Ruthless*—where did that word come from? I'm not sure, but here is an intriguing thought. What if it came from the story of Ruth in the Old Testament? Remember Ruth. In the Hebrew Bible, she is the symbol of love and loyalty, thoughtfulness and faithfulness. She is one who puts others before herself and expresses tender concern for Naomi, her mother-in-law. She is a beautiful example of humility.

Remember that it was Ruth who said those famous words: "Whither thou goest, I will go; and where thou lodgest, I will lodge: thy people shall be my people, and thy God my God" (Ruth 1:16). In Ruth we see the epitome of loyalty to another, the symbol of unselfish love. To be *ruth-less* then must be the opposite of that. To be ruth-less is to be "without the spirit of Ruth," and that was the problem with the disciples that day as they quarreled over position! They had forgotten their Bible. They had forgotten the spirit of Ruth. Their pride was ruth-less, and that was their problem. Maybe it is our problem too!

Deep down, the disciples knew it. They knew that ruthless pride wouldn't really fit in his kingdom; and that's why when it was exposed, they were reduced to silence!

Second, They Were Silenced by Their Bitter Self-Centeredness

I guess those two things go hand in hand, don't they: ruthless pride and bitter self-centeredness. J. Wallace Hamilton, talking about the danger of self-centeredness once said:

> We like [praise] even when we know we don't deserve it. . . . and, as someone has said, we dislike it only when we hear it bestowed too much on others. Bishop Berry used to say that if a man can enjoy hearing his predecessor praised or his competitor complimented, he is qualified as an authority on the doctrine of entire sanctification. (J. Wallace Hamilton, *Ride the Wild Horses* [Westwood, N.J.: Fleming H. Revell, 1952], p. 28)

I once had a professor who said: "There is only one Sin" (with a capital letter). He would point out that there are lots of other sins that are manifestations of that one big sin, but "there is only one big Sin," he would say. Then he would pause for dramatic effect and say, "The one big Sin is idolatry, the worship of self rather than God, the sin of putting yourself and your wants ahead of God and his will." He would go on to show how the scarlet sins like hurting other people or lying or cheating or stealing were really symptoms of the larger Sin, idolatry, putting yourself before God and everybody else.

What do you think? Was my professor on target? Is our big problem that we want to worship self rather than God?

One thing is for sure: Self-centeredness is dangerous! It blinds us and will not fit in the Kingdom.

Third and Last, the Disciples Were Silenced by Their Hostility

They were quarreling, bickering, arguing. Even as Jesus, the Master of Love, moves toward the cross, his closest followers, his most intimate friends are seething with hostility. There is a certain pathos about this. They have heard him preach and teach love, they have sensed his spirit of humility and compassion, they have seen his acts of loving-kindness; and yet they seem here to have missed his main point. Jesus had to go to the cross to get their attention! There on the cross he shows them and us that love—not hostility, that love—not self-centeredness, that love—not ruthless pride, that love is life as God meant it to be. This quarreling of the disciples bothered Jesus very much. Hostile bickering has no place in his kingdom. When are we going to learn that?

He stops and deals with their bickering quite seriously. Notice how it reads in Mark 9. It says "Jesus sat down [and] called the twelve!" In Jesus' time, teachers would walk about teaching, instructing, pointing out truths along the way; but when they wanted to say something authoritatively, something of supreme importance, they sat down! Remember the Sermon on the Mount. Jesus goes up on the mountain and sits down, and then he preaches it. Here Jesus sits down and teaches them authoritatively again to be servants, to be humble, to be trusting, and to be loving.

Jesus is very disturbed by their ruthless pride, their self-centeredness, their hostility, and for good reason. Maybe it's because he knows that these same things, magnified, blown up to a larger scale await him in Jerusalem. A scant few days later these same destructive attitudes, ruthless pride, bitter self-centeredness, and bickering hostility, nailed Jesus to a cross! These attitudes put him there! It's still happening today! Every time we demonstrate these attitudes, we are crucifying God's truth, and somewhere along the way we have to answer for it.

But the good news is that ultimately, in God's own time, his truth and his love will win the day; and then ruthless pride, bitter self-centeredness, and bickering hostility will be reduced to a shameful silence!

4

The Blindness of Jealousy

John said to him, "Teacher, we saw someone casting out demons in your name, and we tried to stop him, because he was not following us." But Jesus said, "Do not stop him; for no one who does a deed of power in my name will be able soon afterward to speak evil of me. Whoever is not against us is for us. For truly I tell you, whoever gives you a cup of water to drink because you bear the name of Christ will by no means lose the reward."

—*Mark 9:38-41*

My good friend Mark Trotter once preached a sermon entitled "Lateral Thinking." He referred to Edward De Bono who says he invented the concept of lateral thinking. De Bono established a school in New York, called it "The Edward De Bono School of Thinking," and started giving seminars on how to think "outside the box," how to think creatively and how to think laterally. He says he came up with the idea of "Lateral Thinking" when he was a Rhodes scholar at Oxford.

One night while he was there, he attended a party in London that ran late; and when he got back to Oxford, he discovered that the gates had been closed. He had to climb two walls to get to his room. He said, "I got over the first wall without too much difficulty. I came to the second wall and noticed it was exactly the same height as the first one. So I had no difficulty with that one either;

except when I hit the ground, I discovered I was back outside the first wall." He had climbed over and across a corner and ended up right back on the outside where he started.

So he tried again, this time paying more attention to the second wall. He noticed that there was a gate in the second wall, and that the gate was lower than the rest of the wall. It also had footholds on it, so he decided it would be easier work to climb over the gate. So, that's what he did. However, when he was astride the top of the gate, it slowly opened. It had not been locked!

Edward De Bono said he learned two great lessons from that experience. Lesson Number One was: "No matter how good you are at climbing walls, you should always pick the right ones to climb." And Lesson Number Two was: "Some walls don't have to be climbed. You can enter through a door no one ever imagined." That, he said, is how he discovered "lateral thinking," solutions that move laterally, and sometimes even backward, until you find the gate that nobody knew existed.

For example, once Edward De Bono was called in to solve a problem for a large corporation. The corporation was housed in one of those tall New York skyscrapers. The building did not have enough elevators. Consequently, there was a huge morale problem because the office workers were so frustrated and angry and impatient because they had to wait so long for an elevator. The corporate leaders tried everything they could think of to solve the problem. They sped up the elevators. They staggered the work hours. They even looked at the possibility of adding more elevators, but nothing worked.

Then they brought Edward De Bono in, and he came up with an ingenious idea that solved the problem immediately. You won't believe what it was. He told them to install mirrors around the elevator doors! The people will see themselves in the mirrors and become so interested in looking at themselves that they won't notice that they are waiting so long for the elevator. And it worked! That is called "Lateral Thinking." Instead of attacking the problem head-on, you move to the side until you find the open gate—or a new way. (Thanks to Mark Trotter, "Lateral Thinking," July 12, 1998, sermon First United Methodist Church, San Diego, California)·

Now, with all due respect to Edward De Bono, the truth is: He didn't really invent "Lateral Thinking." Jesus used that approach more than two hundred years ago. For example, Jesus used his parables to not only help us see things more clearly; but more often than not, his parables were told to help us see things differently! The key to understanding the parables is to look in each case for the surprise, to get into the sandals of those original listeners, and to get in touch with the place where their eyebrows went up in shock and they found themselves exclaiming: "O my goodness!" and then saying, "Did I hear that right? Did you hear what he said? Surely he didn't mean that! Run that by me again!"

Let me give you a "for instance." In the parable of the prodigal son, when Jesus tells about the remorseful, penitent, defeated, ashamed prodigal returning home from his riotous living in the far country, those early listeners just knew what was coming next: "O boy, is he ever gonna get it now! His daddy is gonna lay into him and tell him a thing or two; or more likely, his daddy is going to say: 'Get out of my sight! I don't know you! You are dead to me. You are no longer part of this family. You chose your bed; you go sleep in it!' " That's what they fully expected Jesus to do in this parable; but surprise of surprises, Jesus astounds them. He doesn't have the father do the obvious. He doesn't have the father use the usual door of vengeance and retribution. No! The father moves laterally and finds a new door called grace and forgiveness, and in that story Jesus shows us graphically that amazing grace is always better and much more beautiful than angry, harsh, condemning judgment.

We see it again in his parable of the good Samaritan. Now, the parable obviously teaches us to help our neighbors; but the surprise here is that the hero in the parable is not a priest, not a Levite, not even a good orthodox layman, but (of all people) a Samaritan! a half-breed! an unclean outcast! The original hearers of this parable were not just surprised; they were absolutely shocked. "What? Did you hear that? Can you believe he said that? A Samaritan? Come on now! This is too much to stomach! He's been out in the desert sun too long!" But, you see Jesus knew exactly what he was doing. He was "thinking laterally." He was moving outside the box; and with that one powerful story, he opened a new door and said: "All people (even Samaritans, even outcasts, and even untouchables), all people are your neighbors!" The people back then believed in loving their neighbors, but they thought their neighbors were only those who looked like them and dressed like them and ate like them, thought like them and talked like them. Foreigners weren't neighbors; they were adversaries—that's what they thought.

But then along came Jesus moving laterally and saying: All people (even Samaritans, even outcasts, even untouchables, and even foreigners), all people are your neighbors. So love them, respect them, include them, value them, honor them, and help them. The people back then were blind to that way of thinking and acting. Unfortunately, some people still today have the same kind of blinders on. They can't see it. But, here comes Jesus, the Great Physician, reaching out to them and to us. He wants to touch our eyes and enable us to see clearly with 20/20 spiritual vision. He wants to touch us powerfully so that from this moment forward we can see, not with the eyes of prejudice or discrimination or bigotry but with the eyes of love.

The scripture lesson for this chapter (Mark 9:38-41) is another case in point. Remember it with me:

John (of all people, John the beloved disciple) comes to Jesus with a bold announcement. With some sense of pride he says to Jesus, "Teacher, we saw a man casting out demons in your name, and we forbade him because he was not following us. We stopped him because he was not one of us. He was not in our group, so we shut him down!" Now, I am sure that John expected Jesus to "pat him on the head" and congratulate him for a job well done, but again Jesus moves laterally and gives a surprise response: "No, no, no . . . Don't do that! Don't stop him! Don't be jealous or resentful of him! If he is doing good work in my name, then he is not against us. He is with us. We are all working for the Kingdom and that's good. He is not an enemy to be silenced; he is a teammate to be embraced."

Here is another one of those poignant moments in the Gospels where the disciples have spiritual cataracts. Their vision is obscured. They just can't quite see it clearly, and sometimes the truth is: Neither can we! Now, if we look at this scripture lesson closely, we can see here three different ways we as modern-day disciples can be so easily blinded. Let me show you what I mean.

First, We Can Be Blinded by Jealousy

The green-eyed monster called "jealousy" can obscure our vision and destroy us. Jealousy is so destructive and so sneaky, and we are especially vulnerable to being tripped up by jealousy in our own field, in our own specialty. If that man in Mark 9 had been doing magic tricks or singing folk songs or forecasting the weather, he would have been no threat to John and the other disciples at all. But when they saw him doing good in the name of Jesus, he had entered their field; and they became jealous and had to stop him. They couldn't stand the thought that he might outdo them in their own specialty.

Dick Milham, one of America's top convention speakers, uses an ancient Lebanese legend to show how dangerous jealousy can be. According to the legend, two shepherds saved the life of a drowning man. After the rescue was made, the man who had been rescued sat on the riverbank and made a startling statement to the two shepherds, "You have shown great courage and saved my life. Now, I have the power to give you a great gift. Either of you may wish for anything you desire, and you will receive it. And the other one will receive twice as much!" At first, the two shepherds thought the man might be crazy; but after he left, they decided that if he did indeed have that power, they should be careful and take it seriously.

One of them turned to the other and said: "You go ahead and wish." He started to, but then remembered that the other man would get twice as much; so he said: "No, you go ahead and wish first." In the beginning, it was like a game. They kidded each other about the wealth; but as time passed, they became more serious. One of them would think, "I'd like a mountain of gold, but he would get two mountains of gold." The other would think,

"I'd like an ocean of diamonds, but he would get two oceans of diamonds." So, the tension grew, the jealousy increased, and the friendship crumbled.

Finally, one night one shepherd could take it no longer. He seized the other by the throat and started choking him, screaming: "You wish! Wish now or I will kill you!" And in that moment, the startled man looked into the jealous face of his one-time best friend; and he gasped, "I wish . . . I wish . . . to be blind in my right eye." So, he was made blind in one eye; and the other man, now blind in both eyes, stumbled in darkness for the rest of his life.

The point is painfully clear: jealousy destroys. They had a wonderful opportunity; it could have been a win-win situation, but they were done in by jealousy. Jesus knew how dangerous jealousy can be; and he was saying to his disciples back then and to us right now: Be bigger than that. Don't be blinded by jealousy.

Second, We Can Be Blinded by Envy

There is an interesting story that comes out of ancient Greece that shows powerfully how destructive envy can be. According to the story, two Greek athletes were very close friends. They were like brothers, and both of them were incredibly gifted athletes. But one of them began to get more recognition, even to the point where the townspeople built a life-sized statue of him to honor him as their number one athlete. They placed the statue on a big pedestal in the center of the town so everyone could see it. The other man became so envious that he couldn't see straight; so envious that every night after dark, he would go out and try to destroy the statue. He wanted to push it off its pedestal and destroy it, and no one would ever know he did it. Finally, he succeeded. He toppled the heavy statue off its pedestal; but it toppled forward and then toppled backwards, and it fell on him and crushed him to death. He was destroyed by his own envy.

Put that over against this. Robert E. Lee was once asked his opinion of a certain man. General Lee responded: "He is a fine and able man, and I commend him to you highly!" "But General," the questioner protested, "don't you know how this man talks behind your back. Don't you know the terrible things he says about you?" "Yes," Robert E. Lee answered, "I know, but you didn't ask how he felt about me. You asked me what I think of him; and I think he is a fine and able man, and I commend him to you highly."

Now that is the spirit in which Jesus wants us to live. It's called unconditional love, and it is the opposite of envy. We can be blinded by jealousy. We can be blinded by envy.

Third and Finally, We Can Be Blinded by Resentment

The man in Mark 9 was doing great things. He was healing people in the name of Jesus, and John and the other disciples couldn't stand that. They didn't like that. They resented it. They were afraid this man might outdo them.

One of the things that I love most about our United Methodist Church is the way we embrace and respect and cooperate with other churches and other denominations. On Sundays when we say the Apostles' Creed and we say we believe in the "holy catholic church," we mean we believe in the universal church; or in down-home Texas language, we mean that we don't think we are the only ones who make up God's church. We gladly join hands with other churches. We don't see the other churches or other denominations as the enemy to be silenced, but as the teammate to be embraced.

I grew up in the Methodist Church and I loved it, but when I got to the ninth grade (maybe it was teenage rebellion), I thought, "Who says I should be a Methodist?" So I went to visit some other denominations just to test the waters. Maybe it was a coincidence, maybe it was a sign of the times; but in every church I visited, somebody got up and criticized other churches and other denominations. One church even said that they were the only ones who would get to go to heaven, and the rest of us were doomed.

I realized something: I had never heard anything like that in the Methodist Church. Our church always spoke of other churches with love and respect and even admiration. In my home Methodist church, the one I grew up in, I never felt any criticism or resentment of other churches; so that insight brought me back home, and I realized I do love being a Methodist because we in the Methodist Church love the other churches. We respect them and embrace them and join hands with them eagerly.

The point is clear:

Jealousy can blind us.
Envy can blind us.
Resentment can blind us.

Those who are doing good things in the name of Jesus are part of us. They are not against us. They are with us. May Christ open our eyes to see that and celebrate that.

5

The Blindness of Self-Importance

People were bringing little children to him in order that he might touch them; and the disciples spoke sternly to them. But when Jesus saw this, he was indignant and said to them, "Let the little children come to me; do not stop them; for it is to such as these that the kingdom of God belongs. Truly I tell you, whoever does not receive the kingdom of God as a little child will never enter it." And he took them up in his arms, laid his hands on them, and blessed them.

—*Mark 10:13-16*

Some years ago a man by the name of Andrew Gillies wrote and published a poignant poem which has become a classic. He called it "Two Prayers." It's one of my favorites because it so beautifully underscores one of the great truths of the Bible; namely that we need to become more childlike. Listen now to these touching words:

Last night my little boy confessed to me:
Some childish wrong;
And kneeling at my knee
He prayed with tears—

"Dear God, make me a man
Like Daddy—wise and strong,
I know you can."
Then while he slept
I knelt beside his bed,
Confessed my sins,
And prayed with low-bowed head,
'O God, make me a child
Like my child here—
Pure, guileless,
Trusting Thee with faith sincere."

I like that poem for a couple of reasons. For one thing it reminds me personally of how much I have learned from our children. They are so special, and they have taught me much over the years. But the Andrew Gillies poem also reminds me of this dramatic scene in Mark 10 where Jesus blesses the children and says, "Truly, I tell you, whoever does not receive the kingdom of God as a little child shall never enter it." How relevant those words are for us today because we in our modern, urbane, "success-at-any-cost" world are so prone to become too tough-minded, too sophisticated, too cynical, too hardhearted, too business-like, too image-conscious, too cold and calculating.

Somehow in recent years, many people in our world have become jaded and harsh and critical of everyone and of everything. For example, a media frenzy was created a few years ago because Michael Jordan changed the number on his basketball jersey. Some news reporters went absolutely berzerk. They bashed him mercilessly. But think about it. In the ultimate scheme of things does it really matter whether Michael Jordan wore 45 or 23 on his Chicago Bulls uniform? Why do we build our heroes up and then take such delight in trying to tear them down?

Then I read an article in the newspaper that absolutely amazed me. A group in Europe is now bashing Mother Teresa! Of all people, the late Mother Teresa? That sweet, dedicated, hard-working, compassionate, committed, saintly nun who gave her life to helping people who were destitute and dying, and they are attacking her? The group is complaining that Mother Teresa used all of her energy to help needy individuals and therefore did not attack the social ills of Calcutta! When I read that, I couldn't help myself. I said out loud, "Give me a break!" Surely, we have better things to do than criticize Mother Teresa.

But, you see, somehow over the years many people in our world have become so heavy-handed, so angry, so suspicious, so derisive, they have lost the quality of childlikeness! They have become so caught up in their own self-importance that they think they have to constantly blow the whistle, sound the alarm, and be the prophets of doom. They want to be the watchdogs of society, and unfortunately, far too many have become attack dogs! They have lost the joy and wonder and innocence of childhood. You can see the problem written large in the worried, anguished look always on their faces.

In a lighter but similar fashion, this is what the disciples were doing in Judea that day. Caught up in their own self-importance, they were "throwing their weight around," swaggering about, acting sophisticated, barking out their commands, "Get back there you kids! Get those children out of here! This is serious business! We don't have time for this! We are doing big things up here! Don't bother the Master! Get back and keep quiet! He doesn't have time for children!"

But when Jesus saw what they were doing. He was displeased, "No! No! No!" he said to them. "Don't do that! Let the children come to me! And remember this," he said, "whoever does not receive the kingdom of God like a little child shall not enter it." Obviously, Jesus is referring here not to childishness but to child-likeness. He probably was drawn to the qualities of genuineness, receptivity, dependence, trust, love, openness, affection, curiosity, energy, enthusiasm, joy, and wonder. All of these are characteristics of children, and they are also characteristic of the Christian lifestyle. Elton Trueblood said it well in his writing called *The Heart of a Child:*

> We tend to glorify adulthood and wisdom and worldly prudence, but the Gospel reverses all that. The Gospel says that the inescapable condition of entrance into the divine fellowship is that we turn and become as a little child . . . tender and full of wonder and unspoiled by the hard skepticism on which we so often pride ourselves. God has sent

children into the world, not only to replenish it, but to serve also as sacred reminders of something ineffably precious which we are always in danger of losing . . . (the quality of childlikeness). Thus, the sacrament of childhood is (always for us) a continuing education.

With that in mind, let's think together for a few moments about the great lessons our children are teaching us. There are many, of course. Let me mention three of them. I'm sure you will think of others.

First, There Is Gratitude

Some years ago in a midwestern town a little boy was born blind. His mother and father were heartsick, but they struggled with his blindness the best they could. Like all such parents, they prayed and hoped for some miracle. They wanted so much for their son to be able to see. Then one day when the little boy was five years old, the community doctor told them that he had heard about a surgeon at Massachusetts General Hospital who was specializing in a new surgical procedure that might just work for their son, that might just give their little boy his eyesight.

The parents became excited at the prospect; but when they investigated further and discovered the cost of the surgery and the travel and the hospital expense involved, they became deflated because they were not people of means at all. In fact, some would call them poor. But word got out in the community, and their church rallied to help them. In a short period of time, the money was raised to send them to Boston for the surgery. On the morning they were to leave for Boston, the little boy gathered his things together, including his tattered little teddy bear. It had an ear chewed off, was missing an eye, and was bursting at the seams. His mother said: "Son, why don't you leave that old teddy bear at home? He's about worn out. Maybe we can buy you a new one in Boston or when we get back." But he said, "No, I need it."

So, off to Boston they went. He held tightly to that teddy bear all the way. The surgeon sensed how important the teddy bear was to the little boy, so he allowed the boy to keep the bear with him throughout all the many examinations prior to surgery. On the morning of the surgery, the hospital staff brought in two surgical gowns, one for the little boy and a smaller version for the teddy bear, and off to the operating room they went, a little blind boy on a stretcher holding on dearly to his beloved teddy bear.

The surgery went well. The doctor felt good about what they were able to accomplish. "I think he will be able to see," said the surgeon, "but we won't know for sure until we remove the bandages in a few days." Finally the day came for the doctor to remove the bandages from the boy's eyes. Miracle of miracles! The little boy could see! For the first time in his life he saw his mother's face; he saw his dad and his doctor; he saw flowers and candy and balloons and the people who had cared for him. For the first time in his life, he saw his teddy bear. It was a joyous celebration!

When it came time for the boy to leave the hospital, his surgeon came into the room. The doctor had grown so attached to the little boy that he had to busy himself with those insignificant gestures that we do when we are trying to surmount a great wall of emotion. They said their good-byes with tears of joy all around, and then the doctor turned to leave. The little boy called him back. "Doctor," the little boy said, "I want you to have this." He was holding out the teddy bear! The doctor tried to refuse, but the little boy insisted, "Doctor, I don't have any money. So, I want to give you my teddy bear to pay you for helping me to see. I want you to have it. It's my way of saying, 'Thanks.'"

The doctor took the teddy bear and shook the little boy's hand and wished him well. For a long time after that on the tenth floor of the White Building of Massachusetts General Hospital, there was on display: a teddy bear, bursting at the seams with a chewed-off ear and one eye. And there was a sign under it written in the hand of that surgeon. It read, "This is the highest fee I have ever received for professional services rendered." (Thanks to Leonard Sweet, *Sweet's Soul Cafe* [Feb. 1995]: 6.)

That little boy was so thrilled that he now could see. So, in response, he gave away his most prized possession. There's a name for that; it's called thanksgiving! Now, of course, that kind of appreciation has to be learned; but when our children learn it and express it so beautifully, it touches us and teaches us the beauty, the power, the importance and the necessity of gratitude.

Second, There Is Love

It was a cold Christmas Eve a few years ago. Will Willimon, dean of the chapel at Duke University, was rushing his family to get in the car. They were running late for the communion service. "Where are the sermon notes? Where is the pulpit robe? Don't forget to turn off the lights. Everybody get in the car and be quiet!" On the way to the church, rushing through the traffic, their five-year-old daughter, Harriet, got sick to her stomach and vomited all over the car. "Great!" Will Willimon thought, "If people only knew what preachers go through." He wheeled into the church parking lot, and jumped out of the car, leaving his wife, Patsy, to clean up the car and get the kids into church; and he thought, "If people only knew what preachers' spouses go through."

His wife, Patsy, led a still unsteady and pale Harriet into the church. They sat on the back pew in the darkness just in case Harriet got sick again. Their son, William, age seven, ran down to the front of the church to sit with his grandparents. Will Willimon threw on his robe, took a deep breath, and joined the choir for the processional. He made it through the first part of the service and the sermon. Then came Holy Communion. Will Willimon's wife, Patsy, came down to the altar to receive the sacrament, but she left five-year-old Harriet on the back pew. Harriet was still so pale and so weak and so sick.

But then something beautiful happened. Seven-year-old William got up and came back to the communion rail. "What on earth is he doing?" wondered his parents. "He's already received communion once. What is he up to?" They watched him race to the back of the church and scoot down the pew toward his sister. He opened his hands revealing a small piece of bread. "Harriet," he said, "this is the Body of Christ given for you."

Without hesitation, little Harriet picked the bread out of her brother's hands and popped it into her mouth and said, "Amen";

and in that moment Holy Communion had never been more holy. Then seven-year-old William patted his five-year-old sister Harriet on the head. He smiled. She smiled. And then he turned and ran back down to the front of the church to rejoin his grandparents (*The Christian Ministry* [July–Aug. 1989]: 47). Think of that. No one else thought about Harriet. No one else thought to include her. No one else reached out to meet her need that day except her seven-year-old brother, William.

There's a name for that; it's called love! What a beautiful thing it is when our children rise to the occasion and teach us once again the power of love, the wonder of love, the miracle of love.

Third and Finally, There Is Faith

What is faith? It's "trusting God come what may." It's committing your life to him and trusting him in every circumstance. My brother, Bob, who is a minister in Memphis, recently shared with me a moving story that makes the point.

A little girl had somehow received a bad cut in the soft flesh of her eyelid. The doctor knew that some stitches were needed; but he also knew that because of the location of the cut, he should not use an anesthetic. He talked with the little girl, and he told her what he must do and asked her if she thought she could stand the touch of the needle without jumping. She thought for a moment, and then said simply, "I think I can if Daddy will hold me while you do it."

So the father took his little girl in his lap, steadied her head against his shoulder, and held her tightly in his arms. The surgeon then quickly did his work and sewed up the cut in her eyelid, and the little girl did not flinch. She just held on tight to her father. That's a parable for us in our spiritual lives and a graphic reminder that whatever we have to face, we can hold on tight to our Father and he will see us through.

There's a word for that: it's called trust or faith. It's surely what Jesus had in mind when he said, "Unless you become like a little child, you cannot enter the kingdom of God." It's surely what Paul had in mind when he said, "I'm ready for anything, for

Christ is my strength." The quality of faith, the commitment to trust in God come what may! The spirit of childlikeness is so important, and our children have so much to teach us. How great it is when they teach us the powerful lessons of gratitude and love and faith!

6

The Blindness of
Mixed-Up Priorities

As he was setting out on a journey, a man ran up
and knelt before him, and asked him, "Good Teacher,
what must I do to inherit eternal life?" Jesus said to
him, "Why do you call me good? No one is good but
God alone. You know the commandments: 'You shall
not murder; You shall not commit adultery; You shall
not steal; You shall not bear false witness; You shall not
defraud; Honor your father and mother.' " He said to
him, "Teacher, I have kept all these since my youth."
Jesus, looking at him, loved him and said, "You lack
one thing; go, sell what you own, and give the money
to the poor, and you will have treasure in heaven; then
come, follow me." When he heard this, he was shocked
and went away grieving, for he had many possessions.
—*Mark 10:17-22*

His name was Oscar. He was a high school student in Memphis,
Tennessee, some years ago. He was an outstanding track athlete.
His specialty was the 800-meter run. His goal was to be the state
champion.

Oscar worked hard for days, weeks, months, for more than a
year preparing himself physically and mentally to qualify for the

State meet—and to win it. He exercised daily, ate all the right foods, got plenty of sleep, ran (nobody knows how many) miles, made all kinds of sacrifices, all with one objective in mind—to become the state champion in the 800-meter run. And when the spring of the year came and the track season began, Oscar was in perfect condition, primed and ready to accomplish his goal—state 800-meter champion. He breezed through the practice meets, easily won the city meet, the district meet, the regional, setting new records all along the way. And finally his big day came—the day of the state track meet and the time for the 800-meter run. Oscar was ready. The gun sounded, and quickly he was out in front. By the end of the first lap, he was so far ahead that it was obvious that he was in a class by himself. As they came around the final turn of the last lap, Oscar was running smoothly like a beautifully tuned machine, moving swiftly toward an overwhelming victory, a stunning performance, and a new state record.

But then something happened that turned Oscar's dream into a nightmare. The crowd was caught up in the excitement of Oscar's great race. The spectators were all standing and cheering wildly. Many of them were leaning over the grandstand rails, photographers were snapping flash pictures; and in all the chaos, Oscar became confused! He thought he had completed the race! He thought they were cheering his victory! He thought he had already won, and he stopped! He stopped ten yards short of the finish line. One by one, the other runners passed him by, and Oscar finished last! All his hopes, work, exercises, discipline, sacrifices went for naught because Oscar stopped short of the finish line. He was so near victory, so near his dream; he was so near, but yet so far!

There was a Roman governor who was conducting a trial some time ago. His name was Pontius Pilate. He sensed that there was something different, unique, special about this prisoner who stood humbly before him. He respected the prisoner. He feared him. He admired him. He could find no fault in him. Pontius Pilate knew that he had the power to set the prisoner free. He held the life of Jesus in his hands, but he washed his hands—and the Son of God was nailed to a cross. Pilate was so near to greatness. He was so near, but yet so far.

There was another man named Judas. He lived and traveled with Christ. Daily, he walked with him, talked with him, ate with him. He heard him preach, listened to him teach, saw his mighty works, felt his love. But when the going got rough, when crisis came, Judas sold him out, betrayed him with a kiss, signed his death warrant—and then he went out and hanged himself. Judas was so near to Christ. He was so near, but yet so far. Now, that phrase pops into my mind every time I read Mark's account of the rich young ruler. Here is yet another person who was "so near, but yet so far." Remember the story with me.

Jesus is on his way to Jerusalem, (indeed, he's on his way to the cross) when the rich young ruler runs up and kneels before Christ. Notice this:

He runs up—a sign of enthusiasm. He kneels—a sign of reverence and respect. Thus, we can assume here that this young man is not trying to trap Jesus with loaded questions (as others tried), but that he is really sincere when he asks, "Good Teacher, what must I do to inherit eternal life?" Jesus answers, "You know the commandments: Do not kill; do not commit adultery; do not steal; do not bear false witness; honor your father and mother." Then the young man answers, "All these I have kept from my youth." Jesus then looks at him with love and says to him, "But you lack one thing: Go, sell what you have and give to the poor, and you will have treasure in heaven; and come follow me."

At this, the rich young ruler turns away and leaves sorrowfully, for he is a wealthy man. Like Oscar, he stops short of the mark. Like Pilate, he washes his hands of Christ. Like Judas, he sells out the Lord. He was so near the truth, so near discipleship, so near eternal life; so near, but yet so far.

This all raises a significant question that each one of us needs to hear and grapple with—a haunting, probing question—namely this: "Are we so near, but yet so far?" We may be church members. We may come every Sunday, but the question still rings forth. The question still begs to be answered. We have already seen that we can hear Christ's teachings and see his mighty works—and still reject him, still stop short, still wash our hands of him, still sell him out, still betray him with a kiss. The rich young ruler was an upright, decent citizen, but he could not make the leap of faith; he could not take the additional step of complete commitment to Christ. He was a good man; but so far as we know, he never became a disciple of Christ.

It has been a source of immense weakness in the church that so many church members have been upright, decent citizens, but have never really gone on to become obedient, sacrificial self-giving disciples of Christ. They are good people who mean well, but the truth is they attend church and serve the church if and when it's convenient. This point is underscored in *Webster's* dictionary because there one of the definitions of the word *Christian* is, strangely enough, "a decent, civilized or presentable person." This is the definition that way too many persons accept, but it is not the biblical definition. To those people who think Christianity is nothing more than being nice, decent, civilized, or presentable, Christ would come and say, "You lack one thing! You are so near, but yet so far!"

We can learn a lot from the experience of the rich young ruler. In his failure, we can learn in a backdoor sort of way the basic characteristics of authentic Christian discipleship and the real priorities of life. There are many. Let me list a few, and I'm sure you will think of others.

First, There Is a Strong Personal Commitment to Jesus Christ

Authentic disciples are personally committed to Jesus Christ. Mom and Dad can't do it for us. Uncle John and Aunt Sue can't do it for us. Grandmother can't do it for us. It's a personal decision, a personal commitment. We have to make our own personal leap of faith and accept Christ as Lord and Savior on our own. And it needs to be unflinching allegiance and an unshakable commitment.

A minister friend of mine, James Ozier, recently had an experience we can all identify with in this technological world in which we live today. He tried to reach his credit card company by phone to ask a simple question. Here's how he describes what happened,

"Recently, I had the need of doing some business with my credit card company; so I called their hot line! What answered was a high-tech info-option recorded operator. It went something like this, 'Hello. This is your automated customer service center. To continue this message, please punch in your account number on your Touch-Tone phone.' I punched.

'Thank you. For account balance verification, please punch 1; to make a withdrawal, please punch 2; to question a charge, please punch 3; to determine credit limit, please punch 4; to speak with a customer service representative, please punch 5; to hear these instructions repeated, please punch 6.' I punched 5. 'Thank you. To speak with a representative please punch in your mailing zip code.' I punched. 'Thank you. To speak with a representative about additional features of your card, please punch 1; to report a lost or stolen card, please punch 2; to ask a service representative about Christmas cash, please punch 3; to hear these instructions repeated, please punch 4; to speak to a representative about another problem, please punch 5.' I punched 5. 'Thank you. So sorry, but you've missed our regular service hours. Please call back tomorrow.' "

The Bible tells us that God is the opposite of that. God is a personal God who is always there for us. He doesn't put us on hold, or disconnect us, or ask us to call back tomorrow. He is a caring, loving, personal God who relates to each one of us in a personal way. But there's another side to that coin. We must relate to him personally; and more often than not, that's where the real rub comes for so many people. They don't want to let God in. They are scared to let him get too close. They choose to keep him at arm's length.

In his book *Dear Mr. Brown* ([New York: Harper & Brothers, 1961], 173-74), Dr. Harry Emerson Fosdick puts it like this:

So many church members are secondhand Christians. Their Christianity is formal, not vital. They have inherited it from their families, borrowed it from their friends, married it, taken it over like the cut of their clothes from the fashion of their group. Their churchmanship is part of their responsibility—not hypocritically professed, they believe it after a fashion—but the profound experiences of the soul which transform character, sustain strength and courage, dedicate life, and make God intimately real, they have not known firsthand. They are Christians by hearsay.

Please don't let that happen to you. Please don't ever be content with a secondhand Christianity. Please accept Jesus Christ as your personal Lord and Savior and make a strong unwavering personal commitment to him as the Master and Ruler of your life.

When he was a young boy, Michelangelo came to a master sculptor, asking to be accepted as a student. As they talked about the commitment involved in becoming a great artist, the master sculptor said to the young Michelangelo, "This will take your life!" Michelangelo replied, "What else is life for!"

Listen! Christ is near us right now, and he is speaking loud and clear to you and me. Can you hear him? He is saying, "Deny yourself, catch the spirit of the dream and follow me." Well, what are you going to do? What are you personally going to do? Are you going to turn away sorrowfully? Or are you going to say, "What else is life for?" Being an authentic disciple means lots of things, but for sure it means a strong personal commitment to Jesus Christ. To do less is to be so near, but yet so far.

Second, There Is a Strong Personal Commitment to the Holy Habits

Not long ago, I was in a restaurant and noticed that one section of the menu was labled "soul food." Listed there were items like black-eyed peas, corn on the cob, mashed potatoes, pork chops, candied yams, and so forth. Don't those sound great? But the truth is that good as those are, the real "foods for the soul" are not black-eyed peas and candied yams. The real "soul foods" are prayer, Bible study, corporate worship, Christian fellowship, and service to others. These are the things that nurture us, develop us, grow us up, mature us, and keep us alive and well and spiritually healthy. These are the holy habits that give us our energy and strength and vitality; and sometimes we forget that, don't we?

Dr. Ernest Campbell tells a wonderful story about a woman who went into a pet store to buy a parrot. She wanted a parrot that could talk. The owner of the store sold her a bird guaranteed to talk. She thanked him, took the bird home, and placed him in a cage. Two days later, she returned to the store to say the parrot had not yet talked. "Did you put a mirror in the cage?" the pet store manager asked. "A mirror?" "Oh, yes," he replied. "Sometimes parrots like to preen themselves in front of a mirror, and that helps them begin to talk." So the woman bought a mirror, took it home, and placed it in the cage.

The next day she returned to the store. No luck. No response. The parrot still had not even tried to talk. "Try a ladder," the manager said. "Sometimes parrots like to climb ladders, and that stimulates them to talk." So the woman bought a ladder and tried that, but still to no avail. Not a peep. The next day she returned again. The parrot was making no progress she reported. "Try a swing," said the man. "Parrots like to amuse themselves on a swing, and that will surely do the trick." Dutifully, the woman bought a swing and placed it in the cage with her bird. The next morning, she came back to the store. "My parrot died last night," she said sadly. "I'm truly sorry to hear that," said the manager. "Did the parrot say anything at all before he died?" "Yes he did," came the reply. "Just before he breathed his last breath, he said, 'Don't they sell food down at that pet store?' "

Ernest Campbell then points out how we readily buy mirrors by which to primp, ladders by which to climb higher, swings by which we seek pleasure. But where is the food for our souls? (Ernest Campbell, *Preaching* [March/April 1991]: 57). If we neglect the real soul food, we starve to death spiritually. It's as simple as that. Authentic disciples have a strong personal commitment to Christ and a strong personal commitment to the holy habits. Don't leave those out of your life.

Third, There Is a Strong Personal Commitment to Love as a Way of Life

There is something very interesting here in the story of the rich young ruler in Mark 10. Did you notice it? When Jesus and the rich young ruler talk about the commandments, they mention only those commandments that deal with our relationships with other people: Do not kill; do not commit adultery; do not steal; do not bear false witness; honor your parents. What do you make of this? The commandments that call for love for God are not mentioned here. Why? Well, simply because this is the best way we express our love for God—by loving other people, by loving his children!

A good friend of mine expressed it well. He said, "When I first became a Christian, I was so excited that I wanted to hug God. Over the years, I have learned that the way you hug God is to hug his people!" He is so right. Remember how Jesus put it, "As you did it to one of the least of these, you did it to me."

Not long ago, Duke University conducted an interesting survey that showed that the people today who are really happy and fulfilled are those who are committed to something bigger than themselves, then have a sense of meaning, purpose, and mission. They are committed to a great cause. Do you want happiness? Do you want fulfillment? Then commit your life to Christ, commit your life to the holy habits, commit your life to love. To do less is to be so near, but yet so far.

7

The Blindness of Selfish Ambition

James and John, the sons of Zebedee, came forward to him and said to him, "Teacher, we want you
to do for us whatever we ask of you." And he said
to them, "What is it you want me to do for you?"
And they said to him, "Grant us to sit, one at your
right hand and one at your left, in your glory." But
Jesus said to them, "You do not know what you are
asking. Are you able to drink the cup that I drink,
or be baptized with the baptism that I am baptized
with?" They replied, "We are able." Then Jesus said
to them, "The cup that I drink you will drink; and
with the baptism with which I am baptized, you will
be baptized; but to sit at my right hand or at my left
is not mine to grant, but it is for those for whom it
has been prepared."

—*Mark 10:35-40*

Many of you are familiar with the name James Baker, the states-
man. James Baker served our country well over a number of years.
He held some of the most prestigious, powerful, and influential
positions in our nation's capital. He was the Undersecretary of
Commerce in the Ford Administration; the Chief of Staff in the
Reagan White House, the Secretary of the Treasury under

Ronald Reagan; and with George Bush, he served as Secretary of State and Chief of Staff.

On February 1, 1990, James Baker was asked to give the keynote address at the National Prayer Breakfast in Washington, D.C. It was a unique morning. Heads of state from three continents and citizens from approximately one-hundred and fifty nations of the world met in the spirit of Jesus Christ to pray together, to talk together, and to get to know each other better. In James Baker's address on that crisp February morning, he said these remarkable and poignant words:

> I am here this morning because I believe that those of us who are put in positions of public trust should not be hesitant to speak about spiritual values. In fact, I believe spiritual values are important in the pursuit of world peace. Power, of course, can be intoxicating and addictive, and few doubt the truth of Lord Acton's words that "Power tends to corrupt, absolute power corrupts absolutely." Over these last nine years, I have had opportunities to participate in the exercise of more power than I would ever have imagined. I have felt the weight of responsibility that that brings, and I have also felt the temptations attendant to it. . . . And I found early on that having a position of power does not bring the fulfillment that many think it does.
>
> Of course, it does bring excitement, . . . [but] having a position of power does *not* bring inner security and fulfillment. That comes only by developing a personal relationship with God, which for me is personified by Jesus Christ. Inner security and real fulfillment comes by faith—not by wielding power in the town where power is king.

Then James Baker said this, "In 1986, I met with a group of diplomats gathered here, . . . [and] one of them asked me what I felt was the most important thing I had learned since being in Washington. I told him it was the discovery that *temporal power is fleeting.*" It doesn't last! James Baker told him about an experience he had early one morning a few years earlier, when he was the White House Chief of Staff. He was entering the northwest gate of the White House in a limousine. Friends were with him. Staff members were with him. Secret service personnel were with him; and as James Baker looked down Pennsylvania Avenue, he noticed a man walking down the street all alone.

The walking man was trudging along, shoulders slumped, the

picture of loneliness. He recognized him. He was the Chief of Staff of a previous administration! "There he was alone—no reporters, no security, no adoring public, no trappings of power—just one solitary man alone with his thoughts." James Baker said that mental picture served to remind him of the "impermanence of power and place. That man had it all—but only for a time." It didn't last. It went away. That mental picture puts it all in perspective for us; and the point is clear: Don't put your faith in power or position or fame. Rather, put your faith where it belongs—in God. There is a verse in Proverbs that puts it like this:

> Trust in the LORD with all your heart,
> And lean not on your own understanding;
> In all your ways acknowledge Him,
> And He shall direct your path.
> (Proverbs 3:5 NKJV)

I don't know if James Baker had a text for his keynote address to the National Prayer Breakfast in February of 1990; but if he had chosen our text for this chapter (Mark 10:35-40), he would have chosen well. Remember it with me. Jesus is heading toward the cross. He has "set his face toward Jerusalem." He has told the disciples what lies ahead. But they don't get it. They just can't see it. They are still thinking about a powerful, luxurious, military kingdom. So here they come—James and John—with an ambitious request.

"Teacher, we want you to do for us whatever we ask. We want you to give us the top two positions in your new kingdom. Grant us to sit, one at your right hand and one at your left when you come into power." Jesus answers: "You don't know what you are asking." You see, Jesus knew that they weren't seeing it clearly. They were thinking about power and position and fame and political clout, while he was thinking about sacrificial love and service. They were thinking about rising to places of prestige; he was thinking about death on a cross. They were thinking about the perks of being rulers in high places; he was thinking about saving the world by being a suffering servant.

So Jesus says to them in effect, "You are talking the talk, but the real question is can you walk the walk?" This is where the famous hymn "Are Ye Able" comes from. James and John answer boldly, "Lord, we are able." End of story and they all live happily ever after. No! Not quite! The other disciples get wind of this (of how James and John are trying to slip in ahead of them), and they don't like it. The scriptures say, "they began to be angry with James and John." So Jesus calls them all together and gives them the lesson one more time, saying "I've said it before, and I'll say it again. In my kingdom, true greatness is not found in fortune or fame, not found in position or power or political clout. Those things are fragile and fleeting. No, true greatness is found in being a servant." That's a hard lesson to learn, isn't it?

J. Wallace Hamilton spoke about this some years ago, and here's what he said:

> We all have the drum-major instinct. We all want to be important, to surpass others, to achieve distinction, to lead the parade. Or—as Carl Sandburg once put it—"We all want to play Hamlet."Alfred Adler, one of the founders of modern psychiatry, names it the *dominant* impulse in human nature; he thinks the desire for recognition, the wish to be significant is [our strongest impulse]. . . . And while we may be provoked with James and John for asking Jesus to put them first—like soldiers holding up the battle until they have made sure of their promotion—we should in fairness admit that in a thousand subtle ways we too have tried to be drum-major" (Hamilton, *Ride the Wild Horses* [Westwood, N.J.: Fleming H. Revell, 1952], 26).

Ambition, in and of itself, is a good thing, a normal part of our makeup. We all want to be important; we all want to be significant. We all want to do our best. So ambition is basically a good quality. It only becomes bad when distorted or misused. When it becomes selfish or ruthless or cruel, then it becomes a spiritual poison. That's what was brewing in the disciple group that day. James and John were saying, "I'm going to get ahead come what may. If I have to elbow other people out of the way, then so be it!" Here it is, the picture of selfish ambition; and again it is not a very pretty picture, is it?

But then Jesus straightens them out. He says, It's OK to be ambitious, but don't be ambitious to promote yourself. Rather, be ambitious to help others! Be ambitious to serve other people.

Selfish ambition is blind and fraught with problems and difficulties. Jesus knew that, and he wanted to teach his disciples that important lesson. Now, let's break this down a bit and bring it closer to home with three thoughts.

First, Blind Selfish Ambition Makes You Arrogant

Tolstoy once told a parable about the danger of arrogant ambition. It's about a man who was told that he could have for his own all the land he could walk around in one day, from sunrise to sunset. The man jumped at the opportunity. He began leisurely enough, glad for his strong legs; but as he walked, the lure for more and more stirred within him. If he walked faster, he could circle more land. The farther he went, the more he wanted. Soon he began to run. He burned with fever. He gasped for breath. But he could not stop. He could not rest. One word, *More*, reverberated in his brain. At last, the sun began to sink, and his legs began to fail him. He threw off his shirt and his boots. His heart was pounding like a drum, but forcing his body to the utmost just as the sun fell beyond the horizon, he lunged forward with his fingertips touching the goal. He had made it. But he had missed it, for he dropped there—dead! They took a shovel and gave him his land, a strip of soil six by three for his grave! Tolstoy's point is obvious. This kind of ambition is blind. It can destroy us! Notice here in Mark 10 that Jesus does not abolish ambition. He redeems it! He says, "Be ambitious to be a servant!"

A few years ago, I heard a delightful story about a little boy who was in a crowded sanctuary one Sunday morning with his grandmother. He was seated next to her. All went well until offering time. As the ushers began to receive the offering, the grandmother began searching frantically through her purse for her offering envelope, but she couldn't find it. She had left her gift at home. Embarrassed, she kept on looking through her purse for something for the collection plate. Sensing her dilemma, the little boy rose to the occasion and said, "Here, Gramma, you take my quarter and put it in, and I'll hide under the seat!"

Now, that's a light treatment of a very significant spirit: the spirit of being ambitious to help others. That's what Jesus is after. The disciples knew it. They knew selfishness and arrogance did not really fit in his kingdom; and that's why when it was exposed, they were embarrassed.

That's Number One—blind ambition makes you arrogant.

Second, Blind Selfish Ambition Makes You Adversarial

That is, it causes you to see everyone else as the adversary—as the enemy, as the competition.

Up to this point, Peter, James, and John had been close friends, partners, buddies. They were the big three, the inner circle, Jesus' closest confidants, his executive committee. But now as they approached Jerusalem and what they thought would be the establishment of a powerful and prosperous kingdom, now in the crucial moment when they thought the prize appointments would soon be handed out, now in crunch time, James and John saw Simon Peter differently. Blinded by their selfish ambition, they now saw Simon Peter as the enemy, the adversary; and they tried to elbow in ahead of him.

Matthew was so embarrassed by the blind ambition of James and John that later when he tells the story in his Gospel, he changes it. He softens it. Do you remember how? He has the mother of James and John make the request. Matthew thought that seemed more natural, easier to swallow because we know how moms are about their boys; but you can't really cover it. James and John were great men, great disciples to whom we owe much; but in that moment their ambition blinded them.

Remember Oscar Wilde's famous story that depicts the devil crossing the Libyan desert. He comes upon a group of people who are tormenting a holy man. They are trying to tempt him and break his spirit, but to no avail. They can't touch him. They can't upset him. They can't ruffle him. He resists every temptation with a great spirit of peace, poise, and serenity. They tempt him with wine, food, beautiful women, money, and worldly pleasures; but the holy man is steadfast, unbending in his commitment. Finally, after watching the tempters for awhile, the devil whispers to them,

"Your methods are too crude, too obvious. Permit me one moment." Then, the devil walks over and whispers to the holy man, "Have you heard the news? Your brother has just been made bishop of Alexandria." Immediately, a malignant scowl of jealousy clouded the formerly serene face of the holy man. Blind selfish ambition makes you arrogant and adversarial.

Third, Blind Selfish Ambition Makes You Apathetic Toward Other People

Some months ago, a nineteen-year-old college student named David witnessed a friend of his attack a little seven-year-old girl. David saw it happening but did nothing. The little girl was molested and strangled to death. David did nothing to prevent or stop the attack. Eventually, the attacker was caught and charged with murder, kidnapping, and assault; but David was not charged with anything. The district attorney said David's inaction "May be a crime in the eyes of God, but not in the eyes of the state legislature."

David's refusal to show any remorse for the child or any regrets for his inaction are revealing—and appalling! He said, "I'm not going to get upset over someone else's life. I'm not going to lose sleep over somebody else's problem. I just worry about myself first!" Then when asked how the experience had affected his life, he had the audacity to say all the notoriety had helped him get dates.

The sad story of David's apathetic approach to life should serve as a warning alarm to us. It is simply not enough (and certainly not Christian) to think only of ourselves and what we want. It is wrong, destructive, and blind to think we are the only beings that matter in the universe. God made us to live in the world as a family, as brothers and sisters who share the same heavenly Father.

The point is clear and obvious: Selfish ambition can blind us. It can make us arrogant. It can make us adversarial. It can make us apathetic toward others. James and John eventually saw the light. The question is, Have we?

8

The Blindness of Exclusiveness

They came to Jericho. As he and his disciples and a large crowd were leaving Jericho, Bartimaeus son of Timaeus, a blind beggar, was sitting by the roadside. When he heard that it was Jesus of Nazareth, he began to shout out and say, "Jesus, Son of David, have mercy on me!" Many sternly ordered him to be quiet, but he cried out even more loudly, "Son of David, have mercy on me!" Jesus stood still and said, "Call him here." And they called the blind man, saying to him, "Take heart; get up, he is calling you." So throwing off his cloak, he sprang up and came to Jesus. Then Jesus said to him, "What do you want me to do for you?" The blind man said to him, "My teacher, let me see again." Jesus said to him, "Go; your faith has made you well." Immediately he regained his sight and followed him on the way.

—*Mark 10:46-52*

In the Gospel of Mark, the story of Jesus' dramatic encounter with Bartimaeus in Jericho takes up only seven verses of scripture; and yet within these seven verses, we see the crux of the Christian gospel in a swiftly drawn portrait of Christian love. As Jesus encounters Bartimaeus here, he portrays for us the ways in which we as Christians are called to love other people. Now, love is difficult to define (as we all know), but it can be demonstrated. And that is precisely what Jesus does here. He demonstrates Christian love, the kind of love needed in our homes, in our marriages, in our friendships, in our interpersonal relationships, with our coworkers, our neighbors, with acquaintances, and even with strangers.

In this powerful story, we see the anatomy of Christian love. Remember the story with me. Jesus is on his way to Jerusalem. He is on his way to the cross when he encounters Bartimaeus. Bartimaeus, the beggar who is blind, is sitting by the roadside in Jericho. And he is doing what he does daily; he is begging for money. Obviously, he has heard about Jesus. Bartimaeus senses that this is his moment, his chance; and when Jesus comes near, Bartimaeus begins to cry out urgently, "Jesus, Son of David, have mercy on me!" The crowd tries to shush him. They think Jesus is too busy and too important to be bothered with the likes of Bartimaeus, this poor, wretched beggar who is blind. But Bartimaeus will not be denied. He will not be shushed. No! He cries out more desperately, "Jesus, Son of David, have mercy on me!"

Suddenly, Jesus stops. He turns around. Somehow, over the noise of the crowd, he has heard the poignant cry of Bartimaeus; and Jesus calls for him. "Take heart, Bartimaeus," the people shout. "Get up quickly; the Master is calling for you!" Then Bartimaeus throws his cloak aside; he springs up and makes his way through the crowd and comes into the presence of Jesus. Notice here that Jesus is not presumptuous or arrogant or possessive. Jesus never romps and stomps on people. He does not force himself on people. He does not pompously pronounce what Bartimaeus needs. No, he is very low-key. Humbly, he asks Bartimaeus the question, "What do you want me to do for you?" And Bartimaeus answers, "I want to be able to see! Master, let me receive my sight!" Then Jesus says to him, "Go your way; your faith has made you well." The scriptures tell us that Bartimaeus then received his sight, and he followed Jesus on the way.

Now, what do we learn from this powerful story? There is so much here. Obviously, we could go in a number of different directions. For example, we could look at the matter of healing, how Jesus healed Bartimaeus and how healing happens today. Or we could focus on the special qualities of Bartimaeus that jump out of this story—his persistence, his perseverance, his boldness, his determination, his sensitivity to the uniqueness of the moment, his faith, his unwillingness to give in to the fear of embarrassment, his ability to seize an opportunity. Or we could point out that in this great story we have the good news of our faith summed up in three points: our need, God's action, our response. Our need—we, like Bartimaeus, are blind. God's action—God can heal us and restore our sight and give us a new vision. Our response—like Bartimaeus, we can follow him on the way.

There is so much here in this great story; but for now, I want us to zero in on what this story teaches us about love. Love is a many-splendored thing. We see that graphically in this touching encounter between Jesus and Bartimaeus. So, let me list for your consideration a few of the qualities of Christian love suggested by this story. I am sure you will think of others.

First, the Bartimaeus Story Reminds Us That Christian Love Means Respecting and Valuing Other People Personally

"Love? What do you mean by love?" shouts the cynic. The word has lost its meaning. We've used it too frequently, too lightly. We've tossed it about for every sort of feeling from the mildest preference to the wildest passion. We love potato chips and we love the Bible. We love pepperoni pizza and Tom Hanks. We love the Rockets, the Astros (when they are winning). We love our children, our churches, and antique furniture. We love our parents and peanut butter. "Do you see what I'm getting at?" cries the cynic. "Love as a concept has lost its identity. Love as a word has lost its definition."

Well, if you ever feel that way, if you ever feel fuzzy and

confused about what love is, then remember Jesus. He shows us what love is really all about. He reminds us that love means respecting and valuing other people. Think about that for a moment: To love is to respect and value. If the word *love* feels overused or worn or misunderstood, then try for awhile putting the word *respect* or the word *value* in its place. You know, it works pretty well: "To love God with all your heart, soul, mind, and strength" means to value God more than anything else in the world. To "love your neighbor as yourself" means to respect and value your neighbor's life as much as you respect and value your own. Tonight when you tuck your children into bed, or today when you say "so long" to someone you love, or tomorrow in conversation with a prized coworker, or whenever you want to express something special to someone you care for, try it. Say, "I value you so much!" and see what kind of response you get.

Jesus valued Bartimaeus personally. He stopped for Bartimaeus. I love that! I want to preach a sermon on the subject "Jesus Stopped!" and in it look through the scriptures at all the places where Jesus stopped what he was doing to help people. Jesus was on his way to the cross, but he stopped for Bartimaeus; and when he stopped that was his way of saying: "You count! You matter! You are worth something! You are valuable! You are important to me, and I care about you personally!" We see something very special here in Jesus and something very special about Christian love, namely, that it is intensely personal.

It is not enough to spout high-sounding words of love into the air. Real Christian love demands that we get up close and personal. Remember in "Peanuts" where Linus announces that he is going to be a doctor when he grows up. Lucy scoffs at this, "You, Linus, a doctor? Don't be ridiculous! You could never be a doctor, Linus. You don't love humankind!" "But I do!" says Linus. "I do love humankind. It's people I can't stand!" Jesus shows us here in Mark 10 that it is simply not enough to love humankind. Our task, our calling, indeed our privilege is to love people, to love specific persons, or to put it another way, to respect and value other people personally. Now, that leads us to a second thought.

Second, the Bartimaeus Story Reminds Us of Something I'm Afraid We Often Forget—That Christian Love Is All Inclusive

Light a candle and it will give its light to all in the room. It is not selective. It shines for all. It includes all, embraces all, and that's the way love is. Love reaches out to do good to all people, even the unlovable.

Remember in the scripture lesson how the crowd in their spiritual blindness tried to silence Bartimaeus? "Be quiet!" they said to him. "Don't bother the Master! He is a busy man. You are just a poor blind beggar! He doesn't have time for the likes of you! So hush up, now!" But, you see they were so wrong, so blind. Jesus teaches us here one of the most important aspects of Christian love. He stops to help Bartimaeus, a poor, blind beggar that no one else seems to care about, and in so doing he underscores for us the beauty of all-inclusive love, the beauty of seeing everyone we meet as a person of integrity and worth.

Recently, I ran across a powerful anonymous parable that I think expresses well what I am trying to say. It reads like this: "A disciple asked the holy man: 'How can I know when the dawn has broken, when the darkness has fled? It must be the moment when I can tell a sheep from a dog.' But the holy man answered, 'No!'

"The disciple then asked, 'Is it then that moment when I can tell a peach from a pomegranate?' The holy man answered, 'No, none of these.'

"The holy man said: 'Until the moment when you can gaze in the face of a man or a woman and say, "You are my brother. You are my sister." Until then, there is no dawn; there is only darkness!' "

First, Christian love means valuing other people personally; second, it is all inclusive, seeing and responding to every person we meet as a brother or sister for whom Christ came and died. Here is a third idea that emerges from this story.

Third, Christian Love Is Not Domineering

Maybe, this is why some of the books we see in our bookstores today bother me. I just can't get in my mind the picture of Jesus rushing to a bookstore to buy a book entitled *Negotiating from Power* or *Winning by Intimidation*. Somehow these ideas seem diametrically opposed to the spirit of Christ. Please notice that when Jesus comes face-to-face with Bartimaeus, he doesn't grab him by the collar and say, "I know what you need! I know what you want." No! Courteously, graciously, gently, humbly, Jesus asks him the question—"What do you want me to do for you?" He lets Bartimaeus tell him what he wants and needs.

I think many married couples make a tragic mistake right at this point. During courtship, they are kind, patient, courteous, thoughtful, and considerate. But then they come back from the honeymoon drawing the battle lines, worrying about who is in control, trying to dominate each other; and they forget that Christian love is never domineering. Jesus shows us that dramatically when he says to Bartimaeus, "What do you want me to do for you?" That brings us to a fourth idea.

Fourth, Jesus' Encounter with Bartimaeus Shows Us That Christian Love Is Self-Giving and Sacrificial

It means to give yourself to other people. It means to go out on a limb for others. Christian love acts in terms of the needs of other people. It's not just something you feel. It's something you do for the sake of others. Bartimaeus was crying for help. Jesus heard his cry and came to the rescue.

Some years ago in a small village in the Midwest, a little twelve-year-old girl named Terri was baby-sitting her little brother. Terri walked outside to check the mail. As she turned back from the mailbox, she couldn't believe her eyes. The house was on fire. So very quickly the little house was enveloped in flames. Terri ran as fast as you could into the flaming house only to find her baby brother trapped by a burning rafter, which had fallen and pinned him to the floor.

Hurriedly, Terri worked to free her brother. She had trouble getting him loose as the flames were dancing around their heads. Finally, she freed him. She picked him up and quickly took him outside and revived him, just as the roof of the house caved in. By this time, firemen were on the scene; and the neighbors had gathered outside the smoldering remains of the house. The neighbors had been too frightened to go inside or to do anything to help, and they were tremendously impressed with the courage of the twelve-year-old girl. They congratulated her for her heroic efforts and said, "Terri, you are so very brave. Weren't you scared? What were you thinking about when you ran into the burning house?" I love Terri's answer. She said, "I wasn't thinking about anything. I just heard my little brother crying!" Let me ask you something: How long has it been? How long has it been since you heard your brother or sister crying? How long has it been since you stopped and did something about it?

Now, don't miss the conclusion of this great story in Mark 10. After Bartimaeus received his sight, look at what he did—he followed Jesus on the way! See what this means? Bartimaeus was so moved, so touched, so inspired, so changed, by the love of Jesus that he wanted to be a part of it. He wanted to take up the torch! He was so moved, so touched, so inspired, so changed by the love that Christ gave to him that he wanted to pass it on! He wanted to go out now and give that love to other people in that kind of way! That is precisely your calling and mine, to love every person we see just like Jesus loved Bartimaeus that day.

9

Looking at Life with Easter Eyes

> After the sabbath, as the first day of the week was dawning, Mary Magdalene and the other Mary went to see the tomb. And suddenly there was a great earthquake; for an angel of the Lord, descending from heaven, came and rolled back the stone and sat on it. His appearance was like lightning, and his clothing white as snow. For fear of him the guards shook and became like dead men. But the angel said to the women, "Do not be afraid; I know that you are looking for Jesus who was crucified. He is not here; for he has been raised, as he said. Come, see the place where he lay."
>
> —*Matthew 28:1-6*

A few years ago, there was an eye-catching ad in a Milwaukee, Wisconsin, newspaper's classified section. In big bold letters the headline of the ad read: "USED TOMBSTONE." Underneath the headline were these words: "Used Tombstone for sale. Real bargain for someone named 'Dingo.' For more information call [phone number]."

Wouldn't you just love to know the rest of that story? Who in the world was this person named Dingo and why did he or she no longer have need for a tombstone? The image of a "used tombstone" may at first glance seem somber or depressing. But think of it again: a used tombstone means that its previous owner no longer has any use for it, doesn't need it anymore. It has become a castoff, an unnecessary item.

This is precisely what the Easter story is all about. The message is clear: The tomb is empty! The stone marker is no longer needed! Jesus Christ has conquered death. Good Friday wasn't a period, wasn't an exclamation point; it was only a comma. The story wasn't finished; the battle wasn't over! Jesus has the last word! Jesus has the victory! Jesus Christ is risen!

Remember the story with me. On the Thursday night before Easter, Jesus was arrested on false charges. He was brutally beaten, rushed through a fixed trial held illegally in the middle of the night, and was declared guilty. The next day Good Friday, Jesus was crucified, and then he was buried in a borrowed grave. On Easter Sunday morning Mary Magdalene trudged in sorrow to the tomb looking for a dead body and found instead a risen Lord. She then ran shouting the good news of Easter to the others, "I have seen the Lord! I have seen the Lord! He is risen!" That night, Easter Sunday night, the disciples gathered behind closed doors to try to figure out what this all meant. Should they believe Mary? Had she really seen him? Had he really resurrected from the dead? They wanted to believe, but it seemed too good to be true.

Then suddenly the risen Lord was with them in that very room. "Peace be with you," he said to them. "Don't be afraid." "It's all right. I'm here." He showed them his hands and his side, and they knew it was really their Lord. He had conquered death. They were filled with joy and relief. And then he said to them, "As the Father sent me so I send you." He then breathed on them and said, "Receive the Holy Spirit!" All the disciples were there, all that is, except Thomas. A week later, the risen Lord returned to reassure and redeem doubting Thomas.

Now, in this amazing story, we see neatly outlined three special ways in which Easter opens our eyes that we may see more clearly:

(1) a great comfort
(2) a great commission, and
(3) a great companionship

Let's take a look at these together.

First, Easter Opens Our Eyes to See a Great Comfort

Easter shows us that there is a comfort and consolation when our hearts are heavy. The disciples were grieving, they were afraid, they were disillusioned. Their hearts were broken. They were filled with despair and confusion and guilt. And then the risen Lord came bringing comfort and consolation and hope, "Be at peace," he said. "Don't be afraid anymore. It's OK, I'm here with you. Death thought it had the last word at Golgotha; but as it turns out, we have the last laugh."

My friend, Rod Wilmoth, wrote a wonderful piece a few years ago about the laughter of Easter. He said:

> There are some marvelous pictures that come out of the Resurrection stories. Can't you just imagine Mary getting together with Jesus later and saying with laughter, "I thought you were the gardener." Or try to imagine those two men walking on the Emmaus Road laughing later with Jesus and saying, "Just think, we were trying to tell you about the one who had died."
>
> It does not end there. Remember how Sir Thomas More . . . joked with the hangman on the way to the gallows because his conscience was clear. He knew he was serving God. He could laugh and joke and smile as he faced death because he knew death was not the end . . . O death, where is thy sting? (Sermon by Rod Wilmoth, March 31, 1991)

A good friend of mine tells about a delightful experience he had some years ago. He was on vacation in England and went one night to see Shakespeare's play, *A Midsummer Night's Dream* in Stratford-on-Avon, which, of course, is the home of William Shakespeare just outside of London. My friend said what made it a memorable experience was that the play featured the distinguished actor Charles Laughton. Laughton played the role of Bottom, the chief comic character in the play. My friend described what happened in the play that night like this:

"In one scene Bottom is supposed to die. Oh my goodness, did Charles Laughton ever die. You thought that Charles Laughton would never finish the death scene. He really knew how to die. He went on and on. He was finally lying on the stage with his chest and stomach resembling an enormous tide of ebbing and flowing just going up and down. You were gasping with him and you thought, 'Will he ever stop?' Finally Bottom died. Charles Laughton played the part so well that the audience applauded. I love what Charles Laughton did. He got up and took a bow!" We can only imagine the response that produced!

They crucified Jesus. They killed him; and yet I can tell you that on that first Easter Sunday, Jesus stepped out of that tomb and took a bow! And now because of the resurrection of our Lord, we know as Christians that that is what you and I will be able to do when we die. This is the good news of our faith, the good news of Easter. This is our comfort and consolation when things are tough, and life is hard, and our hearts are heavy.

Sometimes the Good Fridays we face in this life threaten to do us in and bury us, but then along comes Easter to remind us that God will ultimately win. Goodness will ultimately win. Truth and love will ultimately win! At Calvary, evil had its best chance to defeat God and couldn't do it. God wins. That's the joy of Easter, and through faith in him the victory can be ours as well! If that doesn't give us strength for the hard times, I don't know what will. One of the great things about the Easter story is that it opens our eyes to see a great comfort.

Second, Easter Opens Our Eyes to See a Great Commission

The risen Lord returned to put the disciples to work, to pass them the torch, to give them a job. Remember Margaret Deeney's poem called "Proud Words." Read it again:

> 'Tis sweet to hear "I love you,"
>   Beneath a giggling moon;
> 'Tis fun to hear "You dance well"
>   To a lilting, swinging tune;
> 'Tis great to be proposed to
> And to whisper low, "I do;"
> But the greatest words in all the world,
> "I've got a job for you."
>   --*Margaret Deeney.*

The good news of the Christian faith is that that's exactly what God says to us—yes, to you and me: "I've got a job for you! You are important to me! You are valuable! You are needed! I have something I want you to do for me that no one else can do. I want to put you to work."

Here's how the risen Lord says it to the disciples of old and to you and me today. He says, "As the Father has sent me, even so, I send you." In other words, take up the cross! Take up the torch! Take up my ministry! Give yourself in sacrifice and service as I have given myself!

There is a fascinating story about Abraham Lincoln during the time of his presidency. On many Wednesday evenings, he would go to hear the preaching at the New York Avenue Presbyterian Church near the White House. Lincoln was leaving the service one night when one of his assistants asked him, "Mr. Lincoln, what did you think of the sermon tonight?" Lincoln thought for a moment, and then he said, "Well, the content was excellent. And Dr. Gurley spoke with great eloquence. It was obvious that he had put a great deal of work into that sermon." "Then you thought it was a great sermon, Mr. President?" "No, I did not say that." "But sir, you said it was an excellent sermon." Lincoln replied, "No, I said the content was excellent and that the preacher spoke with eloquence. But Dr. Gurley on this night forgot one important matter. He forgot to ask us to do something great!"

Jesus didn't make that mistake, did he? He asks us to do something great. He asks us to do the greatest, the most important thing in the world: to take up his ministry of sacrificial love. "As the Father sent me to give myself for you," he said, "even so I send you to give yourself for others."

Third, Easter Opens Our Eyes to See a Great Companionship

Easter gives the promise of God's constant and continuing presence with us in all the circumstances of life. In John 20, Jesus promises the gift of the Holy Spirit to always be with us and to always watch over us. Remember how it reads, "He breathed on them and said to them, 'Receive the Holy Spirit.' "

Some years ago, Julia Ward Howe was talking to Charles Sumner, the distinguished senator from Massachusetts. She was telling him about one of his constituents who needed his help and encouraging him to get involved in helping this person. The senator answered with a tone of exasperation, "Julia, I am a United States senator. I've become so busy I can no longer concern myself with individuals and their problems." To that, Julia Ward Howe said, "Charles, that is really quite remarkable. Even God himself hasn't reached that stage."

Indeed he hasn't. God cares about you and me personally. He knows your name and mine. He knows our joys and sorrows, our defeats and victories, our agonies and our ecstasies. He knows our prayers before we even pray them. He is nearer to us than breathing. The hymnwriter put it like this:

> He lives, he lives, salvation to impart!
> You ask me how I know he lives? He lives within my heart.
> --Alfred H. Ackley, 1933

These are three of the greatest gifts of Easter:

(1) a deep and abiding comfort when our hearts are heavy,
(2) the awesome commission to continue Christ's ministry, and
(3) the "blessed assurance" of his constant companionship, which we can always count on.

By the miracle of God's grace, these Easter gifts can "open our eyes" to the abundant life Christ came to give us.

Epilogue I

O Say Can America See?
The Demoralizing of America

He has told you, O mortal, what is good;
and what does the LORD require of you
but to do justice, and to love kindness,
and to walk humbly with your God?
—*Micah 6:8*

I don't want to be overly dramatic or overly emotional in this epilogue, and I certainly don't want to be partisan; but I would like to be very personal and very candid because I want to think with you about "The Demoralizing of America." That phrase, "The Demoralizing of America," has a double meaning. It means that we as a nation are in danger of losing our morals and our morale, in danger of losing our virtue and our spirit, in danger of losing our goodness and our soul.

I once read about a woman who phoned her TV serviceman and complained that something was wrong with her television set. The serviceman asked if there were any visible signs or symptoms. "Well, the newscast is on right now," said the lady, "and the reporter has a very long face." The serviceman replied, "Look, lady, if you had to report what's happening these days, you'd have a long face too!" Indeed so. No matter what your political affiliation or stance may be, news reports in recent years are demoralizing for all of us. Ongoing investigations, incessant accusations, impeachment hearings, drug abuse on the rise, more and more violent crime, the shaky stock market, and the menace of terror-ism aimed directly at Americans both at home and abroad. All these things do indeed sap our spirits and give us heavy hearts and long faces.

The truth is that there are many people in our country today who look at what's been happening in our nation in the last few decades, and they feel like things have turned upside down and that we are plunging down a steep and dangerous road with "no steering wheel."

Now, let me hurry to tell you that I am an optimist by nature and by faith, and I am an optimist about our country and strongly believe that we are going to come out of this. I love America! I love the dream of freedom in our nation. I love it that we are "the land of opportunity." I love our spiri-tual roots, our heritage, and our mission. And I genuinely believe that America is the greatest nation to ever grace the face of this earth. I wouldn't want to live anywhere else. So I'm not one of those pessimists or cynics who believe that we have lost the steering wheel. I do, however, see some treach-erous bumps in the road. They are too glaring to miss. I do see some dangerous potholes that can indeed throw us out of control if we don't soon learn how to grab hold of that steer-ing wheel again and get safely past them and back on the right track.

I mention three of these dangers that in my opinion are con-tributing greatly and dramatically to the demoralizing of America. Now, I put a footnote here. It is not my intention to place the blame on any particular party or on any particular political admin-istration or any particular political leader. It is my intention to remind us that we are a family as the American people. We are all in this together, and it is high time for us in the American family to unite and stand tall and address these three dangers creatively and redemptively. It is not too late. In all three instances, the pen-dulum (over the years) has swung too far, and we need to swing it back. Three dangers that are demoralizing America! Are you ready? Here is danger number one.

First, We Are in Danger of Losing Touch with Goodness

In our efforts to be tolerant (which is commendable), we have let the pendulum swing too far and consequently find ourselves in peril of forgetting the moral absolutes, the spiritual laws of the universe, the things that make America great—morality, virtue, integrity, truth, compassion, goodness. "We are in a moral quandary as a nation right now . . . We don't know what goodness is anymore . . . That which once seemed to define the American character has somehow slipped from our grasp" (Brian Bauknight, "What About American Character?" 3 July 1994). Some blame it on the breakdown of the traditional family. Others blame it on the Supreme Court. Still others blame it on the church or the entertainment world or on what has been called in recent years the "Epidemic of Me-ism."

Teresa Heinz referred to it recently as "Continental Drift." She wrote, "Much of what we do in life is not intended to come out the way it does. The actress Mae West probably put it best when she said of herself, 'I started out as Snow White, but then I drifted.' That's what so often happens in life. Things turn out differently than we intended. We make certain assumptions. We forget to worry about details and we drift. But when it comes to (goodness) . . . drift is something we cannot afford. We cannot afford to be inattentive, for we are drifting and not in the direction we intended!" (Excerpts from a speech quoted in the *Pittsburgh Post-Gazette*, 26 June 1994, sec. E, p. 1).

One of the sad consequences of our moral drifting is that we have not connected our young people to the strong faith heritage of America. We have not taught them how deeply rooted in biblical faith was the birth of our nation. This was demonstrated recently by Jay Leno. He was doing his "man on the street" interviews one night. He asked some college students a few questions about the Bible. "Can you name one of the Ten Commandments?" he asked. One student replied, "Freedom of speech?" Then Jay Leno asked another college student, "Can you complete this sentence? 'Let he who is without sin . . .'" Her response was, "have a good time?" Jay Leno then turned to a young man and asked, "Who, according to the Bible, was swallowed by a whale?" The young man smiled with confidence and said, "Oh, I know that one—Pinocchio."

Now, we laugh at that, but the hard reality is that many people today have a hole in the moral ozone. They know nothing about our Western moral tradition. They are morally confused. They are not spiritually mature enough to tell right from wrong.

Some years ago, Paul Harvey did one of his popular "The Rest of the Story" broadcasts. He told the true story about an older man who was a great admirer of democracy and public education. He had a great dream to bring those two things together in the creation of a new public college where the students would practice self-governance. There would be no rules or regulations. The goodwill and judgment of the students would run the college. After years of planning, the school was finally opened, and the older man was overjoyed. But as the months went by, the students proved time and time again that they were not the models of goodness and discipline and good judgment that the man had envisioned. They skipped classes. They drank to excess. They wasted hours in frivolous pursuits.

Then one night fourteen students disguised themselves with masks, filled themselves with alcohol, and went on a rampage that ended in a brutal brawl. One student hit a professor with a brick, and another used a cane on his victim. In response, the college's trustees met in a special meeting. The older man, now eighty-two years old and very frail, was asked to address the student body. In his remarks, he recalled the lofty principles upon which the college had been founded. He said he had expected more—much more— from the students. He even confessed that this was the most painful event in his life. Suddenly, he stopped speaking. Tears welled up in his failing eyes. He was so overcome with grief that he sat down, unable to go on.

His audience was so touched that at the conclusion of the meeting the fourteen offenders stepped forward to admit their guilt. But they could not undo the damage already done. A strict code of conduct and numerous onerous regulations were instituted at the college. Now, that college went on to become one of the great universities in America, but at that moment the older man felt heartsick. His experiment didn't go the way he had planned. Why? Because he took for granted the one essential ingredient necessary for any democracy's success—the virtue and goodness of the people. Those young students weren't spiritually mature enough to realize that only a good and virtuous people can secure and maintain their freedom. A short time later on the fourth of July, the man died. Engraved on his tombstone were these simple words:

Thomas Jefferson
Author of the Declaration of Independence
and Father of the University of Virginia

Now, as Paul Harvey would put it, "you know the rest of the story."

Speaking about this, Jeb Bush said, "Mr. Jefferson's setback at the University of Virginia in the 1820s reflects today's threat to our own larger experiment in self-governance—a national experiment in which success or failure will ultimately be determined by our goodness and virtue. Virtue is indeed the oxygen of a free society. As it fills our lungs we become a people of strength . . . Without goodness and virtue . . . we become strangled and weak" (Jeb Bush, "Virtue and the Free Society," *Imprimis* 26, no. 4 [April 1997]. Reprinted by permission from *Imprimis*, the monthly journal of Hillsdale College.)

In the 1820s, Alexis de Tocqueville came to America from France because he was so fascinated with the greatness of our country. He wanted to know what really made the dream work.

A quotation that is frequently attributed to Tocqueville, but that has been used and adapted over the years from an unknown source, goes something like this: "I looked for the greatness of America in her fields and did not find it there. I looked for the greatness of America in her industries and did not find it there. I looked for the greatness of America in her churches and there I found it. America is great because she is good, and if America ever ceases to be good, she will cease to be great."

In May 1987, newscaster Ted Koppel gave the commencement address at Duke University. He surprised his audience. He didn't talk about politics or international problems. No. He chose to speak on a subject that he thought those graduates needed to hear and think about most of all—morality! Personal morality! And when he finished, he received a standing ovation! In that speech, Ted Koppel said this:

> We have actually convinced ourselves that slogans will save us: "Shoot up if you must, but make sure you use a clean needle"— "Enjoy sex whenever and wherever you please, but always make sure you do it safely." The answer is "No" a thousand times "No." Not because it isn't cool or smart or because you might end up in jail or dying in an AIDS ward if you do—but just because it's wrong! We've spent 5000 years as a race of human beings trying to drag ourselves out of the primeval slime by searching for truth and moral absolutes. And in purest form, truth is not a polite tap on the shoulder; it is a howling reproach. What Moses brought down from Mount Sinai were not the Ten Suggestions. They were the Ten Commandments!

That day at Duke University, Ted Koppel was saying something we all need to hear—namely that the hope of our nation (and our world), the only hope, is that we take seriously the truths of the Bible, appropriate them to our lives, and live them daily. It's important to remember that God's laws and commandments are not given to us to put us in straitjackets, but rather to help us live life to the full. They are not to hinder us, but to help us. Life is better when we love God and other people. Life is better when we are honest and loyal and truthful and kind and caring. God knew that—and that's why he gave us the great truths of the Bible to live by. The point is clear: We've got to swing the pendulum back to goodness because the goodness of the people is the lifeblood of a free society.

Second, We Are in Danger of Becoming a Society of Splinter Groups

We have (in my opinion) way too many polarized cliques, separated tribes, and vested interest groups who are concerned only about "feathering their nests," pressuring for the interests of their particular group with little or no concern for what is good for the nation, what is best for the country. As someone put it recently: "We have always been E Pluribus Unum, but these days we seem to be more *pluribus* than *unum*." Too many groups today forget that the *U* in *USA* stands for *United*. It may sound like a platitude, but as "cliché-ish" as it may sound, it is still profoundly true: "United we stand, divided we fall."

Now, I understand that we need groups to represent the varied interests of our people. I understand that, but I also know that there are times when our vested interests and our partisan politics need to give way and take a backseat to what is best for the nation. I want us to be a united people, not a polarized people, not a fragmented people. Dwight D. Eisenhower put it like this, "A people that values its privileges over its principles soon loses both."

From the beginning, one of the things that has made our nation great has been our strong sense of community responsibility. The Church, at its best, serves as the "Conscience of Society." The Church reminds us that *no one of us is an island*, that we should work not only for our well-being but also for the well-being of our neighbor. Love, respect, service to others—these make freedom possible and the nation great. No matter the cost, we not only think of our welfare, but are concerned about the welfare of others. In other words, we've got to swing the pendulum back from the proliferation of splinter groups because we are all in this together. "United we stand, divided we fall."

Third, We Are in Danger of Swallowing the Mistaken Notion that Freedom *of* Religion Means Freedom *from* Religion

The people who believe this seem to think that religion should be avoided and eliminated from American life, and their position gets pushed to ridiculous extremes. For example, in November of 1991, a state supreme court threw out the sentence of a murderer who killed a seventy-year-old woman with an ax on the grounds that the prosecutor had unlawfully cited biblical law to the jury in his summation.

A few years ago in California, a fourth-grade girl was told by her schoolteacher that she could not wear a cross on her necklace.

In Illinois recently the word *God* was discovered in a second-grade phonics textbook. The second graders were told to strike it out. The seven-year-olds were told that it is against the law to mention God in a public school.

A town in the Midwest not long ago blocked a private Catholic hospital from erecting a cross on its smokestack because, said members of the city council, some local residents would be offended.

And then look at what's happening in the entertainment world. Noted film critic Michael Medved is so concerned about it that he recently helped to create a video documentary entitled *Hollywood Versus Religion,* in which he shows how the movie industry has changed over the years and how they now seem to go out of their way to take potshots at religion.

In earlier days, religious leaders were portrayed as strong heroes like Spencer Tracy in *Boys Town,* but today most religious leaders are portrayed as weak and wimpy and narrow-minded and sometimes even evil. He says that he doesn't think there is a conspiracy concerning this. They haven't come together and said: "Let's shoot down religion." Rather what we have is a small creative community who use the giant screen as their "Bully Pulpit" to press their agenda, which is namely to get all of us to talk like they talk and to think like they think and to act like they act.

When questioned about this, they will say: "Oh, we are not a thermostat; we are a thermometer. We don't set the climate, we just register the climate." Well, let me tell you something—don't you believe that for a minute! They are setting the climate, and it is a climate not favorable to religion. They think freedom of religion means freedom from religion, and they are wrong! A college professor in one of our Western states went to his son's high school graduation. He later said he disagreed with every single word spoken by the guest speaker, and then he said this, "We have to listen to the most heavy-handed dogmatism. Then suddenly (they say) the Constitution is violated if an agnostic hears the word *God*. . . . This is absurd. If we have to put up with things we don't agree with, why is only God excluded? Let's at least keep the playing field level."

Indeed so. Now, please don't misunderstand me. I know that we have great diversity in our nation. I know that we are multicultural and multiethnic. I know that we now have more than twelve hundred different religious groups in our country. I know that there is a need for respect and understanding with regard to our religious differences. But I also know about our faith heritage as a nation and that a nation's identity is shaped by morality, and morality comes from faith.

How can we debate big ethical issues like nuclear arms or the death penalty or drug addictions without reference to religion? How can American children be truly educated without any reference to our spiritual heritage? It's impossible! We need some common sense here. So much of who we are goes back to the great lessons of the Bible. So much of the civilizing process is rooted in our doctrines of faith. So many of our present-day laws go back to the Ten Commandments. And so much of the best of what we are (in my opinion) goes back to the life and teachings of Jesus.

The point is this: We've got to swing the pendulum back to goodness and unity and faith. Goodness, unity, and faith—if you stop to think about it, that is a great synopsis of our text for this chapter: What does the Lord require of you, but to do justice, and to love kindness, and to walk humbly with your God?

Epilogue II

O Say Can America See?
The Answer for America

Just then a lawyer stood up to test Jesus. "Teacher," he said, "what must I do to inherit eternal life?" He said to him, "What is written in the law? What do you read there?" He answered, "You shall love the Lord your God with all your heart, and with all your soul, and with all your strength, and with all your mind; and your neighbor as yourself." And he said to him, "You have given the right answer; do this, and you will live."

—Luke 10:25-28

What is the answer for America? There is so much to be concerned about these days. The problems seem so huge, so complex, so overwhelming, and so unending.

In the last thirty years, we have seen:

a 560 percent increase in violent crime,
a 400 percent increase in illegitimate babies,
a quadrupling of divorces,
a tripling of the percentage of children living in single-parent homes,
a huge increase in teenage deaths,
a drop of 75 points in the average SAT scores of high school students,
more drug use, more alcohol abuse,

more robberies, more assaults, more drive-by shootings, more rapes, and more murders, and more terrorism.

And now more recently, we have been sapped and demoralized by:

ongoing investigations of the White House,
impeachment hearings,
newspaper stories that we have to hide from our children,
feeling that we must "mute" the TV news when the children walk into the room.

William Bennett expressed it like this:

The facts alone are evidence [enough]. But there are other signs of decay, ones that do not so easily lend themselves to quantitative analyses. What I am talking about is the moral, spiritual, and aesthetic character and habits of a society—what the ancient Greeks referred to as its ethos. And here, too, we are facing serious problems. For there is a coarseness, a callousness, a cynicism, a banality ,and a vulgarity to our time. . . . [In addition] there is the ongoing, chronic crime against children, the crime of making them old before their time. We live in a culture which at times seems almost dedicated to the corruption of the young, to assuring the loss of their innocence before their time.
    This may sound overly pessimistic or even alarmist, but I think this is the way it is. And my worry is that people are not unsettled enough. I don't think we are angry enough. We have become inured to the cultural rot that is settling in . . . we are getting used to it, even though it is not a good thing to get used to. . . . People are experiencing atrocity overload, losing their capacity for [moral] shock, disgust and outrage. A few years ago, eleven people were murdered in New York City within ten hours . . . it barely caused a stir. Shortly after that, a violent criminal, who mugged and almost killed a 72-year-old man and was shot by a police officer while fleeing the scene of his crime, was awarded $4.3 million [because the police shot him]. Virtual silence . . . Senator Moynihan calls this "defining deviancy down" . . . And in the process we are losing [our] once reliable sense of civic and moral outrage. (William J. Bennett, "Redeeming Our Time," *Imprimis* 27, no. 7 [September 1998]: p. 3. Reprinted by permission from *Imprimis,* the monthly journal of Hillsdale College.)

What is the answer? What is the answer for America? Now, I don't want to be presumptuous or overly bold, but I want to "take a shot" at this. Somebody needs to say something. Let me begin with a parable:

Once upon a time, there was a little boy with a bad temper. He would lose his temper and say or do cruel things to his friends and even to members of his own family. His father became concerned about this and decided that he should teach him a lesson. His father gave the boy a bag of nails and told him that every time he lost his temper, he was to hammer a nail in the back fence. The first day the boy had driven thirty-seven nails in the back fence. Then it gradually dwindled down. He discovered it was easier to hold his temper than to drive those nails into the fence.

Finally, the day came when the boy didn't lose his temper at all. He was so proud! He told his father about it, and the father suggested that the boy now pull out one nail for each day that he was able to hold his temper. The days passed, and the young boy was finally able to tell his father that all the nails were gone. The father took his son by the hand and led him to the fence. He said: "You have done well, my son, but look at all the holes in the fence. The fence will never be the same. When you say things or do things that are mean or cruel, they leave a scar behind. You can put a knife in a man and draw it out. You can say you're sorry, and you can even be foregiven, but the wound is still there; the scar is still there."

Now, the point of that parable is this: Life has consequences. We have to live with the consequences of our actions. If we do bad things, bad consequences come back to haunt us. Let me be blunt about this. In America in recent years, we have lost touch with goodness. We have endorsed violence and obscenity and perversion and dishonesty and wrong priorities. We have trusted expediency rather than character. We have worried too much about the next election and not nearly enough about the next generation, and now we are living with the scars: We are living with the consequences.

William Bennett put it like this:

> Right now we are playing a rhetorical game in which we say one thing and we do another. Consider the following:
>
> We say that we desire from our children more civility and responsibility, but in many of our schools we steadfastly refuse to teach right and wrong.
>
> We say that we want law and order in the streets, but we allow . . . violent criminals to return to those same streets.
>
> We say we want to stop illegitimacy, but we continue to subsidize the kind of behavior that virtually guarantees high rates of illegitimacy . . .
>
> We say we want to encourage virtue and honor among the young, but it has become a mark of sophistication to shun the language of morality.
>
> We say we want goodness in the land, . . . but instead of according religion its proper place, much of society ridicules and disdains it and mocks those who are serious about their faith. (William Bennett, "Redeeming Our Time," *Imprimis,* pp. 6-7)

And now we are living with the scars; we are living with the consequences.

What is the answer? Well, the answer is crystal clear to me. We have got to get back to what made America great in the first place. From the beginning, America believed intensely that it was a nation under God. We must get back to living by the laws of God. We have got to get back to living in obedience to the Ten Commandments. We need to let what's happening in our nation today be the "two-by-four" that gets our attention and brings us back to the spiritual laws of the universe.

You see, God didn't give us the Ten Commandments to rain on our parade. No. He gave us the Ten Commandments to tell us clearly how things work, how life holds together, how God meant life to be. Anyone who is awake enough to "smell the coffee" can easily see that life is better when we love God and other people; life is better when we respect our parents and guide our children and tell the truth; life is better when we are honest and faithful and kind and gracious in all our relationships. That's the way God meant it to be, and life just works better for us when we live daily by these dependable spiritual laws.

Think of it like this. Just as we know, without question, that there are certain scientific laws we can count on, and just as we know, without question, that if we break these natural laws, we suffer the consequences even so there are also dependable spiritual laws in our world. These dependable spiritual laws are spelled out for us in the Ten Commandments; and when we break them, we suffer the scars, we suffer the consequences.

You see, we don't really break the Commandments. We talk about breaking them, but we can't really break them because they are unbreakable. Whatever we do, they remain intact. We are the ones who are broken when we disobey them. For example, if I climbed to the top of the church spire and jumped off, I would disobey the law of gravity; but I would be the one broken, not the law of gravity. It would still be there, just as strong and dependable as ever. I would not have broken the law; I simply would have proved it.

In like manner, if I choose to disobey the Ten Commandments, I'm the one who is broken. These are not the "Ten Highly Tentative Suggestions." They are our spiritual and moral roots. They are the unshakable, unchanging spiritual laws of the universe, the spiritual laws of God; and they are as valid for us now as they were for Moses and the people of Israel, and indeed for all people who have lived or ever will live on the face of this earth. Jesus summed up the Ten Commandments like this, "Love God with all your heart, soul, mind, and strength; and love your neighbor as yourself."

Now, let me take the teachings of the Ten Commandments and the sacrificial love of Jesus and show you how they are the answer for America and the hope of the world. Interestingly, the Ten Commandments can be outlined in three basic groupings: Loyalty to God, loyalty to the family, and loyalty to others.

(1) The first four commandments call for loyalty to God. No other gods, no graven images, no taking of the Lord's name in vain, and remember the Sabbath to keep it holy.

(2) Commandments five and seven call for loyalty to the family. Honor your parents and be faithful in marriage.

(3) The other four commandments six, eight, nine, and ten, call for loyalty to other people. Don't kill, don't steal, don't lie, don't covet. The answer for America and the solution for all our problems can be found in these three themes:

> Be loyal to God,
> Be loyal to the family, and
> Be loyal to other people.

Let's take a look at these one at a time.

First, Be Loyal to God

Have you seen the new generic greeting card? Birthday, Anniversary, Halloween, Easter—it fits every occasion. On the outside is printed, "Generic Greeting Card." When you open it up, it says, "Whatever!"

Many people go through life like that, just giving their allegiance to whatever the latest fad might be. But these first four Commandments grab us by the scruff of the neck and say, "Wait a minute! That will not work! You can't chase every new wind that blows. God is the one and only Lord of life! Put God first! Give your allegiance to the one true God or suffer the consequences." The real truth is that in recent years we in America have drifted away from God and away from goodness; and we have, like lost sheep, followed a "Generic Whatever Theology" rather than staying close to the good Shepherd. We have been so afraid that we are going to offend somebody that we have neglected the only One who can save us, and now we are living with the scars; now we are living with the consequences. Dostoyevsky reminded us that when we eliminate God, "Everything is permissible."

We are now seeing everything!

One consequence is this. While the world still sees America as the land of opportunity and as the leading economic and military power on earth, this same world no longer sees us with the same moral respect it once did because we have drifted away from God and goodness. We must turn back to God. We must!

Recently, I ran across a wonderful African story. It is called "A Father's Return." It's about a man who considered himself so lucky because he had a wonderful wife and four healthy sons. The oldest son was called Keen Eyes because he could follow tracks through the jungle better than anyone. The second son was named Sharp Ears because he could hear better than anyone. The third son was known as Strong Arms because of his great strength. The fourth son was a little baby.

One day the father disappeared. He was gone all day, and when night fell he still had not returned. They discussed where he might be—in the jungle, up in the hills, at the festival in the next village; but no one did anything. The next day passed and the next. Then a week. Sometimes the sons wondered out loud where he might be, but no one did anything, and after a while they did not talk about it any longer.

But then one morning the baby spoke his first words; and he said, "Where is our father?" The older brothers were jolted by the baby's question. "Maybe we should go look for him," they said. They started out at once. Keen Eyes led them deep into the jungle following his father's tracks that only he could see; but then the trail stopped, and he said, "We must give up." "No," said Sharp Ears, "I can hear the sound of our father over there." He led his brothers deeper into the jungle toward the sounds which at first only he could hear. Suddenly, they saw their father. He was holding a fierce leopard at bay with a spear. Strong Arms ran ahead and tackled the leopard knocking the vicious animal away from his father. The frightened animal turned and ran away.

The father then returned home with his sons. When the story was told, everyone in the village bragged on the three boys and praised their courage and their skills. But the fame went to the boys' heads and they began to argue among themselves about who was the most responsible for bringing their father home. "I led us on his trail," said Keen Eyes. "Yes, but you lost the trail; and I'm the one who heard him deeper in the jungle," said Sharp Ears. "Oh yes, but I'm the one who fought the leopard," said Strong

Arms. And on and on went the debate among the three brothers.

Finally, they asked their father to settle it. "You all did very well," said the father. "But I must tell you that it was not you, Keen Eyes, and not you, Sharp Ears, and not you, Strong Arms. The one who truly brought me home is here." He picked up the baby, and everyone smiled because they remembered that it was the baby who spurred them to action. It was the baby who said, "Where is our father?"

Now, I want to ask you to be very quiet for a moment and listen very intensely. Can you hear it? I can! I can hear the children of America saying, "Where is our Father? Where is our Father?" The children of America (of all ages) are starved to death for God. They are hungry for the redemptive spirit of Jesus Christ. Now, if I were to rewrite that old African folk story, I would have the boys lost in the woods, not the Father. We are the ones lost in the jungle, not the Father.

Everywhere we look we see the pain, the lostness; but really it all comes from one source, namely, that since the end of World War II we have become so permissive, so fuzzy about what is right and wrong, so wishy-washy on ethical matters, that we are in danger of losing our morality as a nation, all because we have left God out of the equation. And now we are suffering the consequences.

Now I know about the separation of church and state. But separation of church and state never meant the elimination of God and the church. It meant, "Let the church be independent of the state so the church can be the conscience of society."

The answer is so obvious. The first four commandments make it clear. We've got to bring our nation back to goodness and morality and integrity; we've got to bring our nation back to God! The first answer is, Be Loyal to God.

Second, Be Loyal to the Family

Commandment number five tells us to honor our parents and commandment number seven tells us to be faithful in marriage; and they both remind us that strong families produce a strong nation and weak families produce a weak nation.

Oh, how we in this modern world need to hear afresh these commandments! Family life is breaking down all around us; and it is tearing our society apart—drug problems, homelessness, sexual promiscuity, violence, abuse, public profanity, emotional illness, crime. These horrendous social problems are strangling the very life out of our world. And most of them are caused by the break-down of family life in our time. Nine out of ten people being held in jail or prison today will tell you that their problems are rooted in a bad situation at home, a destructive, often abusive, family life.

There once was a boy named Bradley. When he was about eight years old, he fell into the habit of thinking of everything in terms of money. He wanted to know the price of everything he saw; and if it didn't cost a great deal, then it did not seem to be worth anything at all to him. But there are a great many things money can't buy, and some of them are the best things in the world.

One morning when Bradley came down to breakfast, he put a little piece of paper, neatly folded, on his mother's plate. His mother opened it, and she could hardly believe her eyes but this is what her son had written:

> What Mother Owes Bradley
> For running errands—3 dollars
> For taking out the trash—2 dollars
> For sweeping the floor—2 dollars
> Extras—1 dollar
> Total that mother owes Bradley—8 dollars

His mother only smiled as she read that, but she did not say anything. When lunchtime came, she put the bill on Bradley's plate along with eight dollars. Bradley's eyes lit up when he saw the money. He stuffed it into his pocket and started dreaming about what he would buy with all that money.

But suddenly, he saw another piece of paper behind his plate, neatly folded. He opened it and found a bill from his mother. It read:

> What Bradley Owes Mother
> For being good to him—nothing

For nursing him through his chicken pox—nothing
For shirts and shoes and toys—nothing
For his meals and beautiful room—nothing
Total that Bradley owes Mother—nothing

Bradley sat there looking at this new bill. He didn't say a word. But then he got up, went over and hugged his mother tightly. He pulled the eight dollars out of his pocket and placed them in his mother's hand. And from that day forward, he helped his mother a lot, but now he did it for love! (*Moral Compass,* pp. 22-33).

I love that story because it reminds us that home is where we receive our first instructions in the virtues. Home provides our first lessons in what is right and what is wrong, and our first brush with unconditional love and our first call to faithfulness. The point is clear: Strong families build a strong and virtuous nation.

The first four commandments call for loyalty to God. The fifth and seventh commandments call for loyalty to the family.

Third, the Rest of the Commandments Call for Loyalty to Other People

Back in the fourth century in France, there was a dashing young soldier named Martin. One day, he was traveling on horseback with his regiment. As they passed through the busy streets of Amiens in France, their swords and spurs and trappings glistened in the sunshine. All the people in the crowded streets stopped to watch them gallop through. Suddenly, one of the soldiers stopped his horse. It was Martin.

Martin noticed something that no one else seemed to see—a beggar sitting beside the road with outstretched hands and a starving face. Martin's heart went out to the beggar. He wanted to help him, but young Martin had no money in his purse. Still he felt he must do something. An idea flashed into his head, prompted by the cold wind that whistled through the air. Martin held up the warm military cloak hanging around his shoulders, he drew his sword and cut the cloak right down the middle. He leaned from his saddle and draped one half of the cloak around the beggar's cold shoulders.

He sheathed his sword, tossed the rest of the cloak over his own shoulders and galloped off after his companions. Some of the soldiers laughed at him and teased him, but others wished they had thought to do exactly what he had done. That night, Martin had a dream. He had a vision of heaven. He saw Jesus with a group of angels. Jesus was wearing half of a cloak. He showed the half cloak to the angels and said, "Look what my friend Martin gave me today!" Martin went on doing deeds of love like that for the rest of his life, and today he is honored as the patron saint of France. His symbol of a sword cutting a cloak in half is a widely loved reminder of the power of sharing and compassion and love.

Now, these final commandments (six, eight, nine, and ten) call us to be loyal to other people, to not kill them or steal from them or lie about them or covet their good fortune; but Jesus came along later to call us to an even higher level of love. The Martin story reminds us of that. Jesus calls us to love every person we meet as if that person were Christ himself in disguise.

Now, let me ask you something. Think about this. If you were a committee of one to select the next person to be featured on the next Wheaties box cover as the top American Moral Champion—not a sports champion—the top American moral champion, who would you pick? Who would you put on the box of Wheaties? My hunch is that it would be somebody who is

> loyal to God and the church,
> loyal to the family, and
> loyal to other people.

Listen, if we in America would bring to the front burner these three principles, if we, as a nation would commit ourselves to these three principles—loyalty to God, loyalty to the family, and loyalty to other people—we could be an inspiration to the world because that's the way God meant life to be.

Study Guide

O Say Can You See? Biblical Stories About Spiritual Blindness

Sally D. Sharpe

This study guide is designed for both individual and group use. When using the book individually, you may choose to read the entire book and then revisit each chapter as you make your way through the study guide. Or, if you prefer, you may take one chapter at a time, reading a chapter and then considering the questions provided for that chapter. In either case, you will find it helpful to record your responses and reflections in a notebook or journal.

When using the book in a group, you may cover one chapter per session, or you may combine or select specific chapters as you choose to shorten your study. When combining two or more chapters for a given session, you may condense the material by selecting from the study questions provided.

Prior to your first session, determine who will serve as group leader. For this study, the leader's role is to facilitate discussion and encourage participation by all group members. To ensure fruitful discussion, *all participants* must commit to reading the designated chapter(s) before each group session. If open discussion is new or uncomfortable to your group, or if your time together is limited, it may be helpful for group members to reflect on the selected study questions prior to the session as well. Some may want to record their responses in a notebook or make brief notes in their books. (Note: Some questions may seem more appropriate for personal reflection than for group discussion. If members of your group are reluctant to discuss these questions, agree to reflect on them individually during the coming week.)

Remember, this is a study *guide*—intended to help lead you on an exploration of the book's primary themes and lessons. The "journey," however, will be different for each group or individual making it. Some will need to take a few detours; others will want to linger at times before moving ahead. Whether studying the book alone or with a group, feel free to adapt the questions as necessary to meet your particular needs and interests or those of your group. In addition to this book, you will need a Bible, a Bible concordance, and a dictionary of the English language. (Groups will need only one Bible concordance.)

May God richly bless you through your study.

Introduction

1. Read Matthew 6:22-23. What was Jesus saying in these verses? Give an example to illustrate his point.

2. How would you define or explain the term "spiritual cataracts"? What are some of the things that can cloud or distort or blind our spiritual vision?

3. Think of a time in your own life when you have suffered from spiritual cataracts—or perhaps even spiritual blindness. What helped to "open your eyes" or "restore your vision"?

4. Do you believe it is possible to have "20/20 spiritual vision"? Why or why not?

5. Read Matthew 5:29. How would you paraphrase this verse? What correlation do you see between this verse and Matthew 6:22-23?

6. What new insight or understanding have you gained from your reading, reflection, and discussion?

Chapter 1. The Blindness of Prejudice

1. Read Mark 8:22-25. How can the healing of the blind man at Bethsaida serve as a parable of the Christian walk and the journey toward spiritual maturity? How is it possible for a person to know Christ and still have "fuzzy vision"? Give an example, if possible.

2. Read Mark 8:27-33. According to this text, how did Peter demonstrate both clear and fuzzy vision?

3. Why did Peter have trouble accepting what Jesus was telling him in Mark:8:31? In what way was Peter "blinded by prejudice"?

4. The author writes that by prejudging how the Messiah should act, Peter "put Jesus in a box." What are some other ways we sometimes put Jesus, or God, in a box? Give an example from your own life, if possible.

5. The author suggests that prejudice can result from closed-mindedness, fear, and laziness. Think of a situation in your life when you were prejudiced toward someone, or when someone was prejudiced toward you. What do you think was the underlying motivation or reason for this prejudice? Was it closed-mindedness, fear, laziness, or something else? How might the situation have been different if you and/or the other person had observed Jesus' instructions in Matthew 7:1-2, 12?

6. Respond to this statement: Peter's unwillingness to accept the necessity of Christ's suffering was a "blind spot" that prevented him from seeing the full truth. How is the fear of suffering often a blind spot to Christians today?

7. Read Matthew 16:24-25. According to these verses, what does faithful Christian discipleship require? Now read Philippians 1:29. What does the apostle Paul mean when he says that it is a privilege to suffer for Christ? Give an example from your own life, if possible.

8. In 1 Timothy we read: "I warn you to keep these instructions without prejudice, doing nothing on the basis of partiality" (5:21). What does it mean to show partiality to a person or group of persons? Do you believe that this can be just as harmful as showing prejudice toward a person or group of persons? Why or why not? Give an example to illustrate your answer, if possible.

9. What new insight or understanding have you gained from your reading, reflection, and discussion?

Chapter 2: The Blindness of Narrowness

1. Respond to this statement: The Christian life is a balancing act of worship (the devotional life) and social action (service), and neglecting one or the other eventually leads to narrow or limited spiritual vision and effectiveness. If possible, give an example from your own life or the life of someone you know to demonstrate what can happen when devotion and service are not kept in balance.

2. What does the author mean by suggesting that "Stop, look, and listen" is a helpful "safety rule for the soul"? Tell of a specific time when you found this guideline to be helpful in your own life.

3. Read Mark 9:2-8. On the Mount of Transfiguration, Jesus talked with Moses and Elijah. What symbolic meaning does this have for us? Why is this realization important to us as Christians?

4. The author says that a mountaintop experience is a spiritual experience in which we encounter the presence of God and the witness of those people of faith who have gone before us; and as a

result of this experience, we are empowered to go down in the valley to serve. According to this definition, what are the essential ingredients or requirements of a mountaintop experience? With these criteria in mind, list as many examples of a potential mountaintop experience as you can (e.g., Sunday worship, personal quiet time, etc.).

5. Read Matthew 14:15-33. Within this passage we read of an occasion when Jesus took time to "stop" and spend some quiet time with God. What happened prior to his withdrawal? What happened afterward? What insights can we gain from Jesus' example? How would you respond to someone who said that corporate worship alone is capable of meeting an individual's need for focused time with God?

6. The author writes that it is important to stop and "let your soul catch up with your body." In addition to spending focused time with God—both alone and with others—what things do you do to "nurture your soul"?

7. So often we tend to go through life with blinders on. Think of a specific time when you were guilty of "tunnel vision"—of focusing so intently on what you were doing that you failed to see what was really going on around you. What was happening? What eventually made you aware that you were missing out on something? How might the situation have been different if you had been fully present to the moment?

8. What have you seen with your eyes that has helped you to perceive the truth—of God's presence, God's love, and God's Word? What does it mean to see with "the eyes of Christ"?

9. Read Matthew 13:14-17. What *spiritual* truth is conveyed by the following words:

> "You will indeed listen, but never understand,
> and you will indeed look, but never perceive" (v. 14)?

Give an example of a time when you listened to God, or God's Word, but did not understand; or a time when you saw evidence of God, or God's truth, but did not perceive.

10. God speaks to us in many ways. How do you listen for God? When, where, and how have you "heard" God speaking to you?

11. Read Psalm 81. Why are we, like the people of Israel, often unwilling to listen to God? What happens when we do not listen to God? In addition to listening, what does God want us to do? What does God promise to do for us in return?

12. Have you ever found that service becomes a desire, rather than an expectation or responsibility, after you have taken time to "stop, look, and listen" for God? Give an example, if possible.

13. Respond to this statement: Before we "go into the valley" to serve, we should take time to "go upon the mountaintop" to be empowered by God.

14. What new insight or understanding have you gained from your reading, reflection, and discussion?

Chapter 3: The Blindness of Arrogance

1. Think of a time when you were reduced to a shameful silence. What happened? If you could relive that moment, what would you do differently?

2. The author opens the chapter with some poignant questions: "If Christ knew what we were doing, would we be embarrassed? If Christ heard what we were saying, would we be ashamed? If Christ knew what we were thinking and feeling, would we be red-faced and speechless?" Of course, Christ *does* see and hear and know all we do, say, and think. Why, then, do you think we often act as if he were not with us every moment? Read Psalm 10. What reasons does the psalmist give?

3. What does arrogance, or pride, have to do with sin? Read the following scripture verses: Psalm 101:5*b*; Proverbs 8:13; Proverbs 16:5; Isaiah 2:17; Isaiah 13:11; Jeremiah 50:31-32; Malachi 4:1. According to these verses, how does God feel about those who are arrogant and full of pride? What are we told will happen to them?

4. Read Proverbs 11:2, 16:18, and 29:23. What always follows arrogant pride? What is the opposite of pride, and what comes to those who possess this characteristic?

5. The author clarifies that sometimes pride is acceptable—even healthy. How would you explain the difference between "unhealthy pride" and "healthy pride"? Give an example of each from your own life, if possible.

6. Read Mark 9:33-37. How did the disciples demonstrate "unhealthy pride"? Now read 2 Corinthians 7:4. How is the apostle Paul's pride in the Corinthians an example of "healthy pride"?

7. Read Psalm 20:7. What does it mean to have pride "in the name of the LORD our God"?

8. Reread the author's explanation of "ruth-less pride" found on pages 34-36. Now read Ruth 1:1-17. How did Ruth demonstrate humility?

9. Do you agree with the professor who said that all sins basically are symptoms of the sin of idolatry (putting yourself before God)? Why or why not? In what ways do we "worship self rather than God"?

10. Reread Mark 9:33-37. The disciples' pride and self-centeredness led to an argument. What does their quarreling reveal about their hearts and attitudes? Why do you think Jesus brought a little child before them? What point was Jesus making?

11. Jesus said we are to be "last of all and servant of all" (Mark 9:35). How does having a servant's heart keep us from becoming hostile toward one another? If possible, tell of a time when you or someone you know avoided or "diffused" a conflict by demonstrating a servant's heart.

12. What do you think the author means when he writes that every time we demonstrate ruthless pride, self-centeredness, or hostility, we are "crucifying God's Truth"?

13. What new insight or understanding have you gained from your reading, reflection, and discussion?

Chapter 4: The Blindness of Jealousy

1. In what way are Jesus' parables an example of "lateral thinking"? Read the parable of the good Samaritan (Luke 10:30-37) and the parable of the prodigal son (Luke 15:11-32). What is the surprising or shocking statement that Jesus was making in each parable?

2. Read Mark 9:38-41. Did John and the other disciples consider the man who was casting out demons to be their "neighbor"? In other words, did they see him through the eyes of love? Why or why not?

3. Why do you think John and the other disciples wanted to stop the man who was casting out demons? What underlying fear might they have had?

4. Fear and possessiveness often lead to jealousy. Remember a time in your own life when you were jealous of someone. Looking back now, why do you think you were jealous? What fear might have motivated your feelings?

5. The *American Heritage Dictionary* defines *envy* as "a feeling of discontent and resentment aroused by another's desirable possessions or qualities, *with a strong desire to have them for oneself*" (emphasis added). With this definition in mind, what *desire* do you

think the disciples might have had, which caused them to be envious of the man casting out demons?

6. Read Proverbs 27:4. What does this verse tell us about the destructive power of jealousy? The author shares several stories to illustrate how dangerous jealousy and envy can be. What personal testimony can you share regarding the destructive power of jealousy or envy?

7. Resentment stems from a feeling of indignation; it is being angry at something one feels is unjust. Why, then, do you think the disciples might have resented the man who was casting out demons?

8. How did Jesus respond to the disciples' jealousy, envy, and resentment? What did he mean when he said, "Whoever is not against us is for us" (Mark 9:40)?

9. Respond to this statement: We Christians often see other churches and denominations as enemies to be silenced, rather than as teammates to be embraced. Read Galatians 3:26-29. What was Paul saying in these verses to the churches in Galatia? What timeless message does Paul have for the church today? In your own words, explain what it means to be "one in Christ."

10. What new insight or understanding have you gained from your reading, reflection, and discussion?

Chapter 5: The Blindness of Self-Importance

1. Read Mark 10:13-16. What did Jesus mean when he said, "Whoever does not receive the kingdom of God as a little child will never enter it" (v. 15)?

2. How would you explain the difference between being *childlike* and being *childish*? What are the qualities of childlikeness? Of these characteristics, which do you think are the most difficult for us to retain as adults? Why?

3. Read the following Scripture verses: Colossians 3:16-17; Ephesians 5:18-20; and 1 Thessalonians 5:18. Why do you think giving thanks—or having a grateful heart—is so important for us as Christians?

4. Paul tells us that we are to give thanks at all times and in all circumstances. What do you think he means by this? How is it possible to give thanks in times of difficulty or tragedy, and how does this help us—as well as those who witness our thanksgiving? Give an example from your own life or the life of someone you know, if possible.

5. Reread the beautiful story of William Willimon's young children and the Christmas Eve communion service (pp. 52-53). What can we learn from young William's act of love toward his sister? Why do you think we adults are often "blind" to the needs of others and consequently fail to seize many opportunities for showing and sharing love?

6. Read Luke 10:25-37. Jesus said we are to love our neighbor as we love ourselves. Yet we, like the lawyer who questioned Jesus, often get caught up in trying to define who our neighbor is. How did Jesus answer that question? (Optional: Tell or write your own contemporary version of the parable of the good Samaritan to answer that question for a modern-day audience. A group might enjoy working on this together—perhaps allowing the story to "unfold" as each person takes a turn adding one or more sentences.)

7. Read Matthew 5:43-46. Here Jesus further clarifies his definition of "neighbor" by calling us to love not only "the lovely" but also "the unlovely"—even those we consider our enemies or persecutors. How did Jesus demonstrate this kind of love in his own life? What are some ways *we* can show love to "the unlovely"? Give an example from your own life or the life of someone you know, if possible.

8. Respond to this statement: Faith is trusting in God, come what may. What would you add to this definition?

9. The psalms extol the importance of trusting in God. According to the following verses, what benefits will we receive when we put our trust in God? List each benefit as you find it. (Psalm 32:10; 33:21; 37:3, 5; 40:4; 52:8; 115:9; 125:1)

10. Read Mark 11:22-24 and Luke 17:5-6. Jesus essentially said that the *quantity* of faith one has is not what is important. What, then, is the key to effective faith?

11. Use a Bible concordance to locate other passages in the New Testament where Jesus talks of *faith*. What common theme or message can we draw from these verses?

12. What does it mean to have childlike faith? Why are we called to have this kind of faith as Christians?

13. What new insight or understanding have you gained from your reading, reflection, and discussion?

Chapter 6: The Blindness of Mixed-Up Priorities

1. In what way does the saying "near and yet so far" describe many professing Christians today? Read Mark 10:17-22. How was the rich young ruler also "near and yet so far"? Why do you think he was shocked by Jesus' response, and why do you think he "went away grieving" (v. 22)?

2. In your own words, how would you define or explain what it means to be a Christian—to be a true disciple of Christ? What are the characteristics or qualities of authentic Christian discipleship?

3. Reread the excerpt from Dr. Harry Emerson Fosdick's book *Dear Mr. Brown* found on pages 59-60. According to Dr. Fosdick, what does it mean to be a "secondhand Christian"? What is lacking in such an individual's life?

4. What does it mean to be personally committed to Jesus Christ? Give an example from the life of a Christian you admire and respect.

5. Is it possible to be committed to Jesus Christ and not have a personal relationship with him? Why or why not?

6. What are holy habits, or "soul foods," and why are they essential to the life of a Christian? Think of a time when you neglected one or more of these soul foods. What effect did this "fasting" have in your spiritual life? Do you think all the soul foods are equally important? Why or why not?

7. In addition to the five holy habits or soul foods the author names, are there others you have found to be fruitful in your own spiritual life? If so, please share with the group.

8. Read Matthew 22:37-39 and John 13:34-35. According to these verses, whom are we called to love? Now read Matthew 5:43-44. How do these verses broaden or clarify our understanding of whom we are called to love?

9. Read Matthew 25:31-40. How do these verses shed light on what it means to be committed to love as "a way of life"? Do you know anyone who faithfully demonstrates this kind of commitment? If so, how has this person's example affected you and others?

10. What new insight or understanding have you gained from your reading, reflection, and discussion?

Chapter 7: The Blindness of Selfish Ambition

1. The *American Heritage Dictionary* defines *ambition* as "a strong desire to achieve something," or "a will to succeed." Ambition itself, then, is perfectly healthy—even necessary for a productive and fulfilling life. Read Philippians 2:3 and James 3:14-16. According to these verses, what makes ambition unhealthy or sinful?

2. Read Proverbs 3:5-6. What specific instruction included in these verses, if followed, can help one to avoid the trap of selfish ambition? How?

3. Read Mark 10:35-45. In your own words, how would you summarize Jesus' response to all the disciples? Using verses 33 and 34, write a one-sentence "job description" for a follower of Christ.

4. What does it mean to be an ambitious servant? Give an example from the life of someone you know, if possible.

5. Someone who is arrogant is overbearingly proud. Use a Bible concordance to locate passages in both the Old and New Testaments that include the words *arrogant* or *pride*. What does the Bible have to say about those who are arrogant and prideful and what will become of them?

6. The author states that selfish ambition makes one adversarial, and he shows how this was evident in the behavior of James and John in Mark 10. Give an example from the pages of history, from the Bible (other than James and John), or from your own life to support the truth of this statement.

7. Respond to this statement: Selfish ambition leads to an apathetic or indifferent numbness toward others. What, then, do you think leads to a selfless compassion toward others?

8. The author suggests that the disciples knew that selfishness and arrogance did not fit in Jesus' kingdom, and that they probably were embarrassed when their own selfish arrogance was exposed. Read 1 Corinthians 13:4-7; Galatians 5:13-14; and 1 John 4:7-11. How do these verses provide further evidence that selfish arrogance has no place in the life of a Christian? What, instead, should be our chief characteristic as Christians?

9. What new insight or understanding have you gained from your reading, reflection, and discussion?

Chapter 8: The Blindness of Exclusiveness

1. Read Mark 10:46-52. How did Jesus demonstrate love in this situation?

2. Read John 15:12. As Christians, we are called to imitate the love of Christ. How would you describe this kind of love to someone unfamiliar with the life of Christ? What Scripture passages would you share to further clarify the meaning of Christian love? (Note: You may find it helpful to use a Bible concordance to locate passages in the New Testament that speak of love.)

3. Look up the words *respect* and *value* in a dictionary. With these definitions in mind, respond to the following statement: Christian love demands that we respect and value others.

4. Read Matthew 5:38-48. How do these verses support the statement that Christian love is all-inclusive? Tell of a time when you extended love to someone you knew was unlikely to return that love. What happened? What enabled you to show love to this person? What known effects did this experience have on you? on the other person? on others?

5. The author writes that Christian love is never domineering. Define the word *domineering*, or *domineer*, and then list as many antonyms for the word as you can. Do these words paint an accurate picture of the kind of persons we are called to be as Christians? What scriptures can you find to support this word picture? (Note: You may find it helpful to use a Bible concordance.)

6. Read the following Scripture passages: Matthew 16:24-25; Matthew 25:31-40; Mark 9:35; 1 Peter 4:10. According to these verses, in what ways are Christian discipleship and Christian love *sacrificial*?

7. Read 1 Corinthians 13. What support or affirmation can you find in this chapter for the author's four major points regarding

the nature of Christian love? What additional characteristics or attributes of Christian love are included in 1 Corinthians 13?

8. Explain the following statement: Christian love is contagious. Give an example from your own experience, if possible.

9. What new insight or understanding have you gained from your reading, reflection, and discussion?

Chapter 9: Looking at Life with Easter Eyes

1. Read the four Gospel accounts of Easter morning: Matthew 28:1-9; Mark 16:1-6; Luke 24:1-5; and John 20:1-18. How are the details of the accounts similar and different? Despite differences among the details, what is the unequivocal message of each account? How would you explain the significance of this message to an unbeliever? What personal testimony could you add to corroborate the eyewitness testimonies of the Gospel accounts?

2. It has been said that Christianity is empty without the empty tomb. What does this statement mean to you?

3. In your own words, how would you explain the great comfort of the Easter story? How has it comforted you personally? Tell of a difficult time when you experienced firsthand the joy of Easter.

4. What is "the great commission"? (See Matthew 28:19-20.) How have you responded to this commission in the past? How do you sense God calling you to respond now—or in the future?

5. After giving his disciples the great commission, what promise did Jesus give them? (See Matthew 28:20b.) How does this promise—this third gift of Easter—enable or empower us to fully realize the other two gifts?

6. Read Romans 8:38-39 and Acts 17:26-28. What insights do these verses give us about God's gift of companionship?

7. This chapter presents three of the greatest gifts of Easter. What other "gifts" would you add to the list? Why?

8. What new insight or understanding have you gained from your reading, reflection, and discussion?

Epilogue I: O Say Can America See?
The Demoralizing of America

1. The author suggests in this chapter that during the past few decades, America has been undergoing a process of demoralization. In your own words, how would you explain what he means by this?

2. Brian Bauknight writes that "we [Americans] don't know what goodness is anymore. That which once seemed to define the American character has somehow slipped from our grasp." Do you agree or disagree with this statement? Why? What evidence or examples can you give to support your answer?

3. What is "moral drifting," and how is it a threat to our society?

4. Reread the story of Thomas Jefferson and the University of Virginia, followed by the comments from Jeb Bush (pp. 88-89). In your opinion, what "moral(s)" or lesson(s) does this story hold for our nation today?

5. Reread the words often attributed to Alexis de Tocqueville found on page 89. Where did de Tocqueville find America's greatness? What is your response to his concluding remarks?

6. The author writes that "God's laws and commandments were not given to us to put us in straitjackets, but to help us live life to the full." What does he mean by this, and how is this possible?

7. How, or when, might "splinter groups" be a threat to our nation?

8. Respond to these words of Dwight D. Eisenhower: "A people that values its privileges over its principles soon loses both."

9. Why does the author attribute the greatness of America to her churches (see p. 91)? In your opinion, what kind of influence does the church today have on our nation? What kind of influence does your own church have in the surrounding community? What more can we, the church, do to teach and encourage a sense of community responsibility and selfless love?

10. How do you respond to the entertainment industry's claim that they are not a thermostat but a thermometer? Do you think that the entertainment industry sets the climate or registers the climate of our culture? Why?

11. How does "freedom *of* religion" differ from "freedom *from* religion"? What evidence can you cite to support the claim that some people in this country would like to eliminate religion from American life? How is such an attempt counter to the very principles on which this nation was founded?

12. Read Micah 6:8. How does this verse serve as a synopsis or summary text for this chapter? What do you think might happen in our country today if we, as a nation, were to observe these requirements?

13. What new insight or understanding have you gained from your reading, reflection, and discussion?

Epilogue II: O Say Can America See?
The Answer for America

1. Reread the words of William Bennett found on pages 96 and 98. What does Bennett mean when he says that we are experienc-

ing "atrocity overload"? Do you agree with his assessment that "we are losing [our] once reliable sense of civic and moral outrage"? Why or why not?

2. Why is allowing ourselves to become desensitized to the atrocities of our violent and vulgar society a dangerous thing? How can we guard against it?

3. William Bennett accuses our culture of committing a chronic crime against children. What is the crime, and why is it so reprehensible? Read Matthew 18:1-6. What additional insights do these verses give you regarding the sanctity of children and their innocence? What did Jesus say about those who corrupt the young?

4. What does the author suggest is the answer for America? What can we do as Christians to help implement this answer to lead our country back to God and God's commandments?

5. The author writes, "We talk about breaking [the Ten Commandments], but we can't really break them because they are unbreakable. Whatever we do, they remain intact. We are the ones who are broken when we disobey them." How have you experienced the truth of these words in your own life?

6. In what way is Jesus' new commandment (Matthew 22:34-40) a summary of the Ten Commandments (Exodus 20:1-17)?

7. The author writes: "Separation of church and state never meant the elimination of God and the church. It meant, 'Let the church be independent of the state so the church can be the conscience of society.' Do you believe it is possible for the church to be the conscience of our society ever again? Why or why not? If so, what needs to happen in order for this to become a reality? How can we initiate and/or participate in the process?

8. Respond to this statement: "Strong families produce a strong nation and weak families produce a weak nation." What can

we do—as individuals, families, and communities of faith—to strengthen the families of our nation?

9. Read Exodus 20:13, 15-17. How do commandments 6, 8, 9, and 10 call us to be "loyal" to other people? Now read Matthew 25:31-40. What "higher level of love" does Jesus call us to? How are we to see others?

10. How can we, as Christians, move our nation toward a commitment to loyalty to God, loyalty to family, and loyalty to other people? How can *you* help to make a difference?

11. What new insight or understanding have you gained from your reading, reflection, and discussion?